STO

ACPL ITEM

P9-ELH-479

DISCARDED

4-21-7

DARE I LOVE?

DARE I LOVE?

JOHN H. McGOEY, S.F.M.

OUR SUNDAY VISITOR, INC.
HUNTINGTON, INDIANA

Nihil Obstat:
Rev. Lawrence Gollner
Censor Librorum

Imprimatur:
✠ Leo A. Pursley, D.D.
Bishop of Fort Wayne-South Bend
June 6, 1974

© Copyright by John H. McGoey, 1971

ISBN: 0-87973-762-x
Library of Congress Catalog Card Number: 74-16464

Published, printed and bound in the U.S.A.
by Our Sunday Visitor, Inc.
Noll Plaza
Huntington, Indiana 46750

762

1868339

CONTENTS

1863333

Preface

Thirty years ago I undertook the celibate life and remain convinced that it is a fulfilling and rewarding one. Celibacy led to love and happiness for me. In recalling the reasons for that being so, it seems clear that my happiness derived from understanding and accepting the basic principles of sex and love. The celibate crisis, reflected tenfold in the crisis of modern marriage, is one of love. Whereas celibates presumed that holiness would mysteriously appear when vows were taken, married people presumed that love would automatically appear when marriage vows were made. In reality, holiness and love, which are the same thing, are not things which merely happen, but high achievements to be understood and worked for.

Like all celibate priests, on ordination, I accepted the commitment to remain unmarried for life. Without knowing precisely how or why, I expected to find adequate compensation in my priestly life for the lack of a full sexual life. I considered my "spiritual life" security enough against turning back or away from the priesthood. I chose the simplest way of discipline, a tight work-schedule which minimized opportunities for exclusive personal relationships, and the leisure for laziness or intrigue. I monitored such relationships as I did have, and lived them from an upper level, as something like a friend but never quite an equal. I failed to see the arrogance of it, nor did I grasp how afraid I was of an equality in which I might not measure up.

The tensions, which I would not feel and seemed outwardly and consciously to carry well, eventually broke me. Circumstances then gave me the opportunity to do some of the thinking I had avoided, in the presence of people I loved, and who loved me enough to tell me when and where they thought I was honestly mistaken, stupid, stubborn or misguided. It was only during serious illness over several lengthy periods, when I had to accept close association and intimate care from women at their most compassionate and loving, that I could no longer escape the "facts of life". I was forced to measure celibacy for its meaning and rewards, against the need everyman has for a mate of his own, for life, in love.

I know that by the time I had to do my thinking, I had learned to think. By then, I knew that one's mind is apt to go out of gear in the uproar of the emotions, that maturity means the ability to think under the emotional impact of infatuation. It was my good fortune to have spent much time alone – in moments of truth, looking at the face of death when everyman is really alone: in war and under Communism in the isolation of China: in the tranquil peace of Harbour Island in the Bahamas; but, even more, in periods of misunderstanding, disapproval and some persecution. Out of this thoughtful solitude grew the conviction, which the years and subsequent experience have deepened, that it is love, not sex, that really matters. I realized that while people need each other desperately, true love is never born of desperation. It seemed that, in one sense, everyman *is* an island, because there is something lacking in the deepest personal union; there is a time in everyone's life when he must learn to live with himself before he can ever live happily with another, or others.

It is in solitude that a man must ask himself the simple question *Dare I Love*? Have I the guts it takes to really love? The truth is always simple. If I ever hope to be fully human, let alone Christian, I have no alternative, no choice. I must love. The sooner people get to loving the better off they are, and the whole world with them. If they will not love there is little hope for them, or for mankind.

A celibate can know as much about love as can any married person. He can know a great deal about marriage too, if he is interested in listening to the innumerable, confused and disappointed married people who come to him wondering where love went, when in reality it never was. He is neither prejudiced in favour of marriage, nor against it, because of personal experience. He can be detached, objective and positive – one of the very few who can.

Herewith I present my ideas about sex and love for what they are worth. But on one thing I insist. No one can be genuinely celibate unless he loves, nor has true love ever led a genuine celibate from his commitment. It is a fact that loving is demanding, but it shows everyman at his very best.

John H. McGoey, S.F.M.

Introduction

There is very little wrong with the world which could not be solved by loving people. However, the emphasis today, in the developed world, is on sexual love, and much more on sex than on love. Yet only in man-woman, or married love is sex a prime factor. The mature person loves God, country, parents, children, brothers, sisters and neighbours – all loves in which the genital sexual factor is of secondary, if any, importance, despite the fact that the human person necessarily loves as a man or a woman. Love is the great achievement of human life. If there must be a choice, it is more human to live without sex than to live without love. But, surely, to understand the more complex power to love one must first understand the simple function of sex.

Humanness comes only in male or female packages. Sex, which is male *and* female rather than male *or* female, is something which both share rather than that each has. Each person can experience only male or female sex; neither experiences singly what only both together can experience and understand. In fact, the opposite sex can be understood only vicariously, through communication. Yet each man and woman can love, can have personal wholeness in loving. The fullness of humanity is reached in the experience of deep personal love.

Marriage is the ordinary avenue to the fully loving life, since man's very existence depends on the genital sex function. His evolution and perfection, however, depend on the genital sex function integrated into the loving life. Nevertheless, single people and celibates are not deprived of the loving life because they choose not to use their genital sex function. Married people opt for love with a full genital sex life; celibates opt for love without full genital sex function. Christian, celibate love forgoes the exclusive sexual relationship of married love to better achieve the loving personal relationships occasioned by its special service to God and fellow man. Thus genuine celibacy is not at cross purposes with human nature but is in the very pattern of loving, the actual direction which the evolution of man is taking.

Loving marriage and celibacy both require the greatest possible understanding of sex. If sex is not understood, it can and will be as much of an obstacle to love in marriage as in celibacy. Human love is interpersonal rather than intersexual. A man's love for a man does not make him homosexual, nor does a woman's love for a woman make her lesbian. Yet one achieves human love only as a sexual person. To achieve love one must have the basic knowledge of male and female anatomy and physiology, and understand the sexual emotions and the relationship of sex to the spiritual dimension of man.

Married love and Christian celibacy both require deep spirituality and full sexuality, integrated into the supreme power to love. Understanding sex is as vital to celibacy as spirituality is to married love. It has been as tragic a mistake to dispense celibates from the one, as to dispense married people from the other. Real people, whole people are essentially sexual, spiritual, understanding, but primarily loving. This is the message of this book.

The material presented in the chapters "Sexual Anatomy" and "The Physiology of Sex" was prepared by E. Dawne Jubb, M.D., F.R.C.S.(C.), on staff at Women's College Hospital in Toronto, and an associate in the Department of Obstetrics and Gynaecology at the University of Toronto Medical School.

The drawings were done by an artist from the Medical Art Department of the Faculty of Medicine, University of Toronto.

CHAPTER ONE

Wholeness

Generations of philosophers were content to define man as a rational animal, heavily accenting the rational. Today, to explain man, naturalists (encouraged by a nearly perfect record of men making monkeys of themselves) capitalize on his remarkable resemblance to his closest living relative, the ape. Konrad Lorenz, the highly respected naturalist, said somewhat enigmatically, "Man is an animal, but he is essentially more than an animal." The simple truth seems to be that while man is no angel, neither is he an animal. He is in a class by himself. He certainly is not an ape who suddenly got smart. He is a unique being, a "human" being, with inherent powers to know and to love. Man's wholeness, his fulfilment, is reached in the development of these two powers. To be understood, *anything* man is must be related to *everything* he is – his entirety. Man is not simply of layer-cake formation – animal plus an added layer to make him human. Rather, he is human throughout; that is, every apparently animal quality in him is actually human.

To maintain his balance, man's power to love must keep pace with his power to learn. Man has concepts which he thoughtfully develops by relating them to prior concepts. He has fantastic ingenuity, despite the fact that at one time he understood thought as little as he still understands love. The institutions of higher learning everywhere testify to his progress in learning. But he also has the power to reflect, has the insight and understanding which precede love. He has the largely undeveloped power to equate the good of others with his own, which is what love does. Animal behaviour can shed some meagre light on the ways of man, but the human psyche is unique and few conclusions drawn from studies of animals can be applied validly to man. Certainly the power to love is strictly his own, and, when exercised, marks him as humanly whole.

Man is not well defined by fragmenting him into his various functions. He is said to have a spiritual life, a physical life, a social and a sexual life, yet he really has one single, human life of many dimensions or aspects. Man's problems cannot be neatly isolated or localized. Whatever ails him, ails the whole person that he is. Professional religious life, as it has been, is a good example of the concentration on one dimension of man to the detriment of the whole person. The intense effort to spiritualize him did, in fact, dehumanize him. To grow spiritually man must grow humanly, personally, be more of a person, a better person. The holier the person the more truly human must he be. Spiritual imbalance makes people less human, whereas true holiness finds them saner, healthier, better developed, more knowing, and, above all, more loving people. The imbalance often seen in men of genius, artists and scientists, does not help them to function better as people, to be more companionable, less islands in the sea of humanity.

The discipline of psychiatry is evidence enough that physical health does not make a whole man. Man's physical well-being is inextricably interwoven with his emotional and spiritual well-being. Abundant food and exercise are not enough to make a man what he ought to be. He needs a true set of values and a high purpose to achieve fulfilment in depth. The most effective psychiatrists are those who believe that such values and motives, to a great extent, lead to the emotional and mental health and therefore to the general well-being of man. The good psychiatrist has a valid concept of the whole person and works toward the development of whole people.

The more impressive, though one-dimensional, are man's material achievements, the less satisfied he seems with his over-all life, the more doubtful about his personal role and identity. He is aware of a personal emptiness as he searches for deeper meaning in life than shelter, food, clothing and physical health. This awareness is a luxury far beyond people contending desperately with sickness, poverty, cold, hunger and discrimination. Affluent man is like the abandoned child adopted into a good home. Despite his relative comfort, he still wants to know who his parents are and why he was abandoned. Man wants to know where he came from and where he is going. He wants to know his relationship to whoever, or whatever, started it all. He knows that he lives and dies but he wants a reasonable explanation for doing so. He feels abandoned, disoriented when there is nothing bigger than himself in which to believe. His power to believe bothers him until he finds an object for it. The desire to look up to, and respect, interested and loving parents reflects his need for love, happiness, the secure continuity of the thread of love from God, through life, to God. Belief is a quality of the whole man. When man is deprived of belief, or deprives himself of it, he is exposed to every kind of superstition. He then believes in no one else, and is beset with doubts about himself, his role, the meaning of his personal life. Man may accept or reject it, but he needs a role, an identity, a purpose of his own. In these he can really live; he is whole.

There is no absolute wholeness for man, in the sense of perfection. His relative wholeness is indicated by the harmonious balance between his knowing and his loving, his search for the truth and his love of the good. He is most truly human and whole when he relates lovingly, thoughtfully and well to others, when he has a solidarity with them, when he belongs. He has then achieved his potential within the human limitations. He is happy. Conversely, the unhappiness of a man, with or without power, wealth and pleasure, is evidence of his lack of wholeness, his state of unloving. Nothing brings man happiness; it originates within himself. Happiness cannot be legislated, precisely because it depends on goodwill, and on man's power over the one person under his complete control, himself. Man can order all his faculties and functions to the happiness of the whole man. The addict, a disoriented man, is necessarily unhappy because of the anarchy in his life. His addiction, whatever it is, is bigger than he is. The happy man is immune to addiction.

Although many aspects of wholeness remain a mystery, the problems of mentally and emotionally ill people are abundantly clear. These are the people who do not relate to other people. Incapable of deeply loving relationships, they are sick, crippled, part people. The physical cripple is the more obvious, but he can and does manage far better than the emotional cripple. Emotional cripples are seldom or easily recognized, and they themselves rarely suspect their condition before it is fully developed, or have the courage to face it when they do suspect it. One is completely horrified by a trip to a veterans' hospital where the broken bodies, the human remnants left in war's wake, can be seen. The frightful cost of war is immediately and shockingly evident. However, the emotional cripples surfacing everywhere today in the affluent society are not the result of war but of the human irresponsibility and unloving, which these days are equated with "peaceful" living. They are cripples simply because they have been deprived of the love needed to inspire them to love others, to grow humanly. No wonder drug or miracle of science touches them; there is no synthetic substitute for love. Unhappy, they substitute pleasure for love and become pleasure's addicts. Even love cannot cure those too damaged to appreciate it, or too rejected to believe in it. They have but the slightest hope of ever living. Genetics cannot eliminate them; birth control or abortion cannot forestall them; suicide is a relief for them. Birth of loving people into loving families, life in a loving and concerned society, is the only answer. The greatest need in society today is for whole people to provide this loving milieu.

History amply indicates that education of itself has never enabled man to act well, to be happy. Certainly the problems of educated man are more complex than those of simpler people. Regardless of the number of solutions it provides for physical, spiritual, economic or social problems, learning hardly touches the problem of man himself. His basic personal problem is the neglect of his power to love. Learning brightens man's mind but loving warms his heart, and his survival requires warmth as much as light. The brightest man in the world is not whole until he loves. Love saves the brightest minds from being caught up in material trivialities which smother them. The ruthless exploitation of one man by another is the incredible price of unloving. Personal and political corruption, the rackets, addictions, greed and tyranny of every kind result from unloving.

Man has fallen just short of believing that education could make him a god. Many bright men once thought it possible to accumulate all knowledge. Now, the more a man learns the clearer it becomes how much he has yet to learn. As Sir Bernard Lovell said so well, "Each new scientific discovery of man makes it clearer how much farther he is from where he thought he was." Currently, man discovers problems faster than he can identify them let alone solve them. He is like the man patching an old inner tube – as soon as one hole is patched, another blows open. Man must now bring his power to love up to the level of his power to learn. He must understand the fantastic difference between sex and love, and their relationship to the process of personal growth. This process requires him to examine sex, which is so involved in human loving that many mistakenly identify them.

Perhaps there was a time when love was not so important for the survival of the race. That day is gone. Affluent civilization has reached the point where loving is indispensable to real progress; is, in fact, the difference between real and imagined progress. A theology of poverty and suffering brought the race through its birth pangs; a theology of affluence and sharing can bring it to maturity. Love is sharing, having the wherewithal to share, wholeness. It is not enough for man to research sex, he must also study human love in depth so that he will be able to understand, teach, learn and live it. He can no longer afford the easy delusion that sex is love, or that love necessarily has any real connection with genital sex. The evolution of man may well depend on love, to make room in the world for living. The unacceptable alternative is the human jungle, teeming with emotional cripples, cannibalizing each other for survival.

When man sees and accepts all that he is, and uses it well in his living, he is whole.

CHAPTER TWO

Sex and Sexuality

The terms sex and sexuality are often used interchangeably. In this book a distinction is made. The term sex generally refers to the genital function; sexuality refers to the quality of maleness or femaleness pervading the whole personality. Sexuality is the inescapable fact of living, from birth to death, as male or female. It is the polarity between male and female, in the physical, physiological, psychological, spiritual and personal human dimensions. One is inescapably male or female in everything one thinks or says or does. The failure to differentiate between the genital function, which one may or may not use, and the inevitable fact of human sexuality with which one lives twenty-four hours a day, is unfortunate. On one hand, this failure has made the necessary genital sexual control seem to demand suppression of the sexual emotions; and on the other hand, the inescapable sexuality has seemed to make genital sex compulsory.

The sexual function is inseparable from the genital organs but not restricted to them. It involves the whole person. Certainly, the most obvious thing about people is their maleness or femaleness. Sexuality is most evident in the genital function but diffuses itself through the whole spectrum of human relations. It expresses itself in all the physical, emotional, mental and spiritual factors and attitudes that can be identified as male and female. People still remain male and female when the genital function has long ceased. Furthermore, sexuality is so related to loving (although it is not to be identified with it) that no human form of affection or love can be expressed other than as male or female. Both compassion for an afflicted fellowman, and love for God Himself, can be expressed only in the way of a man or a woman.

The Judeo-Christian heritage carried with it some contempt for man's undoubted physical relationship to the animal. The things of the mind, spirit and immortal life were stressed almost to the exclusion of the things of the emotions, body and mortal life. The "flesh" was begrudgingly tolerated as "lower nature". Continuing reference to the warring of the spirit against the flesh, and the flesh against the spirit, all but split man's personality, and helped little to reconcile these inseparable parts of man to his essential unity. Bodily functions were ignored if possible, sex was unmentionable, and sexuality considered animal, while the glories of the mind were sung without restraint. Certainly the idea of being first cousin to an ape shocked the Victorian much more than the scandal of evil in man's personal life. This nearly successful repudiation of human sexuality, and the refusal to discuss sex with the tolerance required for understanding any vital function, created the atmosphere for the sexual permissiveness which now exists.

There is great pressure on contemporary man to face and accept his sexuality as fully as he does his intellectuality. Such acceptance will permit the genital function to find its rightful place, and allow its real limitations to be established. The normal role of sex in serving rather than dominating interpersonal relationships would then be determined by true love rather than dictated by sexual passions. Thus, either the use of genital sex or abstaining from it could be recognized as equally loving. It is precisely when love governs the actions of man that sexual pleasure finds its correct place in the ordered life of the happy man or woman, single, celibate or married.

Personal happiness determines the role of sex, eliminating the unnecessary sexual frustration so prevalent in both marriage and celibacy. Clearly sex is as vital to celibate happiness as it is to the happiness of the married person. There is never a need to exaggerate or minimize the importance of sex in the lives of the loving. Genital sex, misunderstood or mismanaged, is as destructive of love in marriage as it is of love in celibacy, because it dominates, or obscures, the person of the loving or the loved.

Knowledge of both genital sex and sexuality, like all knowledge, comes through the senses. The anatomy and physiology of sex, while admittedly the mere beginning of the sex education so basic to understanding sex and love, must be completely familiar and precisely known. To this end the next two chapters of this book are directed. Though they may be superfluous for some readers, the knowledge they contain is indispensable to understanding subsequent things which are not nearly as obvious.

CHAPTER THREE

Sexual Anatomy

Sex is the material of chastity, both celibate and married. Ignorance of sex by those in either state is equally deplorable. Celibates choose to forgo for life the full genital function; married people choose to live a full sexual life. It is inexcusable that anyone be encouraged or allowed to undertake either way of life without a thorough knowledge and understanding of sex. Such knowledge must include both male and female sexual anatomy.

Confrontation with their sexual organs comes earlier and easier to boys than to girls, for from infancy they have handled these organs each time they have gone to the bathroom. Girls require a more studied recognition of their sexual organs, which are normally invisible to them. For females, until recently, ignorance of their sex organs has frequently been considered a virtue.

Reference to the male and female genitals by the common use of vulgar terms originated in ignorance of the correct terminology for the organs, and in religious and cultural denigration of things sexual. This is generally avoided when parents and teachers use the correct names for sex organs in speaking even to the youngest children. The easy use of the right names makes possible the open and intelligent discussion of sex and its functions required for proper development and maturity, and removes much of the superficial mystery from the subject.

Curiosity about sex is in no way morbid but quite normal and healthy. In the best interests of all, it should be satisfied, as all genuine intellectual curiosity should be, with correct, factual information.

The pictures accompanying this chapter could conceivably cause some emotional turmoil in one unfamiliar with the material. However, nothing should excuse the detailed study and understanding of these pictures. The measure of the upset is clear evidence of the need for the knowledge available through them.

MALE GENITAL ANATOMY.

Penis
Cylindrical organ composed of erectile tissue and covered with loose, hairless skin. It is traversed longitudinally by a central canal, the urethra, which serves to transport the urine from the bladder, mucous lubricant from Cowper's glands, and semen from the seminal vesicles to the exterior. The resting state of the organ is flaccid and freely mobile (spongy erectile tissue is empty and soft), and approximately 4 ¼ inches in length. In the erect state, spongy tissue is filled completely with blood, causing penis to be rigid in a stationary position, with its long axis running upward and outward at an angle of about 45 degrees from the anterior abdominal wall. The erect penis is about 1 ½ inches in diameter and 6-7 inches long.

Glans Penis
Very sensitive cap on the outer end of the penis, also traversed by the urethra.

Prepuce (foreskin)
Fold of very loose, wrinkled, hairless skin surrounding the glans penis, but not attached to it. Circumcision is the operation removing this fold of skin.

Scrotum
Sac of hairy skin attached below and behind the penis, containing the two testicles.

Testicle
Male sex gland which produces the germ cells (spermatozoa) and the male sex hormone testosterone.

Seminal Vesicle
Sac interiorly situated behind and below the bladder, for storage of spermatozoa.

Prostate Gland
Large gland at base of bladder which secretes fluid and mucus in which sperm are carried to the outside during ejaculation.

Cowper's Gland

Tiny mucus-secreting gland below prostate which discharges mucus into urethra to pass through the glans penis to act as lubricant for intercourse.

Littre's Glands

A series of small mucus-secreting glands opening individually into the penile urethra.

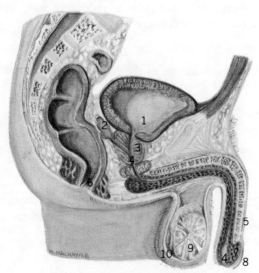

1. bladder
2. seminal vesicle
3. prostate gland
4. urethra
5. penis
6. anus
7. glans
8. prepuce (foreskin)
9. testicles
10. scrotum

Figure A

FEMALE GENITAL ANATOMY.

Vulva
External female genital organs, that is, all that is visible in Figure C.

Labia Majora
Two folds of hairy skin, covering fatty tissue.

Labia Minora
Two thin folds of mucous membrane (soft, moist tissue) next to the inside borders of the labia majora, which meet anteriorly to cover the clitoris like a hood. Deep under these thin folds are two masses of erectile tissue called the vestibular bulbs.

Clitoris
Analogue or equivalent of the male penis; cylindrical organ of erectile tissue approximately one inch long and ¼ inch in diameter, covered by the anterior part of the labia minora.

Glans Clitoris
Very sensitive cap on the end of the clitoris.

Hymen
An incomplete membrane of thin mucous, elastic tissue, extending from the base of one of the labia minora to the base of the other, across the entrance to the vagina. The opening in the centre is of varying sizes. The hymen is often not elastic enough to allow sufficient stretching without tearing, to accommodate the erect penis at first intercourse, and occasionally it is so rigid as to prevent completely the entrance of the penis. Hymenectomy is the name of the operation to enlarge the opening through the hymen into the vagina.

Bartholin's Glands
Small glands situated deep in the tissues beneath the posterior end of the labia minora. They produce mucus which is deposited near the opening into the vagina at its posterior end, to act as a lubricant during intercourse.

Skene's Glands

Tiny glands in the tissue about the urethra which produce mucus deposited at the opening of the vagina at its anterior end, also acting as lubricant during intercourse.

Vagina

Hollow tube of soft muscular tissue attached to the cervix above (inside), and continuous with the vulva below (outside). Its resting state is collapsed with front and back walls of tube touching. The front wall is approximately 3 ½ inches long, the back wall approximately 5 inches long. The vagina's diameter is very variable; it is narrowest at rest, widest (at least 4 inches) during delivery of a baby. The direction of the canal, about 45 degrees from the horizontal, extending back and upwards when standing, matches the angle of the erect penis.

Uterus (womb)

A hollow, pear-shaped organ with very thick muscular walls. Lower end is called the cervix (neck of the womb) and protrudes slightly into the vagina. The lining of the uterine cavity, the endometrium, is very responsive to variations in sex-related hormone levels; it is the tissue in which a fertilized ovum (egg cell) implants, and from which it gets its support at the beginning of a pregnancy. This same lining becomes the menstrual flow when it is sloughed off and drains through the vaginal opening each month that no pregnancy takes place.

Fallopian Tubes

Two muscular tubes extending from the sides of the top of the uterus, sideways, and out to the ovaries. Their length is about 4-4 ½ inches, diameter about ¼ inch. The tube transports egg cells from the ovary to the cavity of the uterus.

Ovary

Female sex gland, almond-shaped, 1 ½ x 1 x ½ inches in size. It houses immature female germ cells called ova and produces female sex hormones, oestrogen and progesterone.

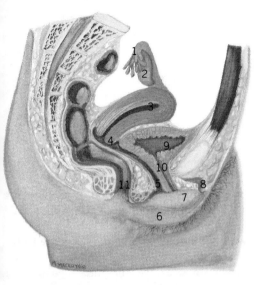

1. fallopian tube
2. ovary
3. uterus
4. cervix
5. vagina
6. labium majus
   (outer lip)
7. labium minus
   (inner lip)
8. clitoris
9. bladder
10. urethra
11. anus

Figure B

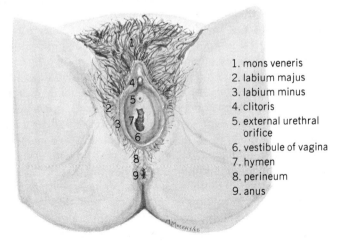

1. mons veneris
2. labium majus
3. labium minus
4. clitoris
5. external urethral
   orifice
6. vestibule of vagina
7. hymen
8. perineum
9. anus

Figure C

CHAPTER FOUR

The Physiology of Sex

As anatomy describes the appearance of the organs of sex, physiology describes their function. The sex of a person is decided at the time of conception. Like the bone structure, the skin colouring, etc., the sex comes from the pooling of the chromosomes from the mature male and female germ cells, the sperm and the ovum.

During the first eight weeks of intrauterine life, the sex of the foetus can be discovered only by the examination of the chromosome makeup of individual cells. By the eighth week the appropriate gonad (sex gland, ovary or testis) is differentiated. By the twelfth week all the sex organs are present in the foetus.

From the twelfth week of intrauterine life to the age of puberty the genital organs remain in an infantile stage, increasing in size as the body grows but not maturing. During this stage, the external sex organs can respond to local, mechanical stimuli in an infantile form of arousal and orgasm response, and often do.

At puberty, the master gland of the body, the pituitary gland, which is located deep in the skull at the base of the brain, initiates stimulation of the sex glands (testes or ovaries) by means of hormones called gonadotrophins. Stimulation of the sex glands results in two basic developments: (i) an increase in the output of the appropriate sex hormones; (ii) maturation of the germ cells in the gonad.

The main male sex hormone secreted by the testes is testosterone. Under the influence of this hormone there is rapid growth and development of the male sex organs at puberty, and their maintenance throughout the life of the man. This hormone also brings out the secondary sex characteristics. Hair over the whole body becomes coarser and more abundant, especially in the armpits, genital region and beard. The larynx enlarges, increasing resonance and deepening the voice. The general body build develops, musculature and athletic inclinations increase.

In the testes the immature germ cells – the spermatagonia – become mature male germ cells – spermatozoa – each complete with a tail for motility, and carrying in its nucleus the particular genetic material this male can contribute to a new person. The mature male germ cells are stored and nourished in the seminal vesicles behind and beneath the bladder.

The main female sex hormone is oestrogen. Under its influence, at puberty, the female genital organs grow and mature rapidly. The labia majora (outer and larger lips) grow large enough to conceal the labia minora (inner and smaller lips). The vagina grows in length, diameter and rugosity, and the ovaries, uterus and tubes increase in size. The female secondary sex characteristics become apparent. The breasts develop, first as buds, deep to the nipples, and then with more generalized enlargement. Hair appears in the genital region and in the arm-pits. Fat depositions occur predominantly in the mons veneris (lower abdomen covering the front of the pelvic bone), but also over the buttocks and thighs. The general body build becomes one of soft contours, broad hips, large thighs and a relaxed musculature.

In the ovary itself, maturation of the primitive female germ cells begins. However, unlike the maturation of the male germ cells (sperm), which is continuous, with mature sperm being stored in the seminal vesicles in huge numbers, in the female only one ovum matures each month, and no mature ova are stored. As soon as the ovum is mature it is extruded from the ovary (ovulation), and it is then propelled through one of the uterine tubes to the uterine cavity. A mature ovum lives only about twenty-four hours after ovulation unless it is penetrated by a viable sperm (conception). If this does not occur, the ovum dies and passes out through the uterus, cervix and vagina. Simultaneously with the ovarian maturation and extrusion process of the ovum, and resulting from hormone stimulation directly related to it, the lining of the uterine cavity (the endometrium) becomes very thick and lush in readiness to supply nutrition and support for the fertilized ovum, should conception take place. Each month without conception, the ovum dies, the endometrial lining becomes superfluous and is sloughed off (menstruation). It is the fragments of this lining and the small amount of blood extruded with it which constitute the menstrual flow.

Once the genital organs have reached a mature state, shortly after the onset of puberty, they are *fully* capable of performing the sexual act. Sexual intercourse, or coitus, takes place when the erect penis is fully accepted by the receptive vagina, where mutually stimulative interaction induces the male and female orgasm or climax. The sexual response or orgasm, spontaneous or induced, can take place in either male or female alone. When it occurs as a result of mechanical stimulation apart from intercourse it is called masturbation.

The genital sexual activity in each sex begins with a local genital lubrication. In the male, a small amount of mucus appears at the tip of the penis. This is not semen, but mucus from the Cowper's glands, and some small (Littre's) glands along the penile portion of the male urethra. Its purpose is to lubricate the tip of the penis to facilitate its entry into the vagina. In the female, at an early stage of the sexual response, the Bartholin and Skene glands near the opening of the vagina secrete mucus for lubrication at the entrance to the vagina. The vaginal walls themselves also secrete mucus to facilitate movement of the penis in the vagina during intercourse.

The second stage of sexual response is one of excitement or arousal. There is a generalized increase of the blood content of the genital organs and the breasts of both sexes. The arterial blood supply to the spongy erectile tissues is markedly and suddenly increased, while the venous exit for the blood is simultaneously slowed, so that the tissue involved becomes stuffed with blood, firm and pulsating. The male penis becomes rigid and elongated like a thick rod, in a stationary position with its long axis running upward and outward from the front of the body. At the same time the scrotum becomes flattened and elevated, the testes are pulled higher in the sac and become larger, the male nipples erect. In the female, the glans of the clitoris swells and the clitoral shaft increases in diameter. The erectile tissue, deep to the labia minora, fills with blood, the labia minora swell up and spread the labia majora in preparation for the entry of the penis. The uterus and cervix enlarge somewhat, are pulled up and back in the pelvis, lengthening the vagina. The vaginal walls become a barrel-like tube increasing in length and diameter. The walls of the outer third of the vagina become more swollen with blood than the rest of the vagina walls, narrowing this part of the vagina like a thick cuff, which grips the penis when it is present. The female breasts enlarge generally and the nipples erect.

When the climax or orgasm is reached a series of rhythmic contractions takes place at intervals of approximately four-fifths of a second, in all the erectile tissue of both sexes. The main feature of the female orgasm is the rhythmic contractions in the outer third of the vaginal barrel and the other engorged tissue surrounding it, including the clitoris. The uterus and cervix also contract at the same rate. The main feature of the male orgasm is a series of rhythmic contractions of the penis matching the vaginal contractions. Similar contractions occur in the seminal vesicles and the prostate gland. These organs expel their contents, which together form the semen, into the uretha where the penile contractions ejaculate it from the penis, with sufficient force to shoot it two feet beyond the end of the penis if it is not contained.

These events in the male and female are accompanied by other body changes. Pulse rate, blood pressure and respiration increase sharply. Most muscle groups in the body go into spasm, hands and feet tense, face contorts, sphincters clamp shut, a rash may appear, and there is often marked sweating.

Following orgasm there is a release of muscle tensions throughout the body, and a release of blood from the engorged areas. The most obvious change in the male is the prompt loss of erection, and the shrinkage of the penis to its normal, unstimulated size. The breast swelling of the female disappears first, then the clitoris and other areas of erectile tissue revert to their usual size.

Physiologically these basic patterns of bodily function remain the same for all intercourse, but psychologically the experiences may feel and be altogether different depending on many circumstances. Sexual intercourse may be an act of deep personal love undertaken in the hope of conceiving a child of that love. It may be a casual visit to a prostitute, or a highly charged, emotionally dominated and irresistible act of passion or lust. These aspects are beyond mere physiology.

The primary purpose of the genital organs, of course, is the production of human beings, the preservation of the species. It is a function vital to the human race but in no way vital to the individual person. It is a voluntary function, and each individual can decide at any time whether he or she wishes to proceed with a genital sexual response or not. That control, which is in every human being, in potential at least, is the basis for responsible parenthood, required not only for conception and birth but more vitally for the proper rearing of children.

The normal state of the genital organs is at rest. Some stimulation is required for their function as genitals. The stimulation can be local, general, physical or psychological. If simple touching of these organs alone were sufficient to stimulate them, they would be automatically stimulated by the clothing, or by the handling for bathing or elimination processes. The usual initiating stimuli are psychic, and dependent on sexual polarity even in autoeroticism. Ideally the response should be elicited by a genuinely loving relationship and carried to completion only in a marriage which is responsible, enduring and securing. Man has that potential, and is most fully human when exercising it.

CHAPTER FIVE

The Sexual Emotions

It is certainly easier to describe than to define the emotions. They register the impact of experience much as the eye registers a picture. They are like inner senses, receiving material from the outer senses, adding the reactions experienced, filtering everything through to the mind for processing into practical judgments. The emotions transfer the outside world to the mind; they connect the flesh to the spirit, trigger the intellect. Stimulated by the emotions, the mind moves into gear. Good judgment requires a well-working set of emotions to supply the material of judgment. The emotions are man's thermostatic controls of pleasure and pain. Through them he comes close enough to the fire to get warm and stays far enough away to avoid being burned, comes close enough to people to be appreciated and stays far enough away to avoid rejection. The emotionally mature man is the one who can enjoy all the pleasure that is good for him and accept none that is harmful, who can accept all the pain that is beneficial to him and reject all that is unnecessary. For such a person pleasure registers as pleasure and pain registers as pain, but he is not dominated by these feelings. The emotions are meant to serve the whole person; they are in no way supposed to run one's life. It is essential to live with one's emotions, not without them, and to have an awareness of one's feelings in general, so that one can identify them specifically. The latter ability indicates a high state of emotional health. One should always experience the feelings normally expected in any given situation. When this is not so, emotional problems of one kind or another are present.

No secondary function of man plays a more important role in his development than do the emotions. They function very much like the amber traffic light, warning of a changing situation to be met. There would be utter chaos at a busy urban intersection if there were not some warning between the red and green lights controlling traffic. The drivers of the cars approaching the intersection from all directions require time to make the proper judgment for passing safely through, or stopping to avoid collision. The amber light provides that time and alerts one to caution, vigilance. The driver then makes the considered judgment to continue or to stop gradually, gently enough to avoid being hit from the rear or dangerously jolting his passengers. The eye registers the amber light; its meaning or impact is registered by the emotions, and the mind makes the judgment about the action to be taken.

The proper role of the emotions is in the order: I feel, I think, I act; *e.g.*, I feel angry, I decide on a beneficial course of action, I carry it out. The emotionally troubled or crippled person short-circuits this procedure into: I feel, I act, with generally unhappy results; *e.g.*, I feel angry, I pick up a knife and stab my adversary. The emotions simply are not built or equipped to do the work of the mind, to make judgments.

Emotional problems are inevitable when anyone permits the feelings to dominate judgment, acting on impulse rather than after due consideration of the situation presented. (Trained reflex actions are not to be considered impulsive.) For example, on meeting a lion face to face one man faints, another screams, another freezes so rigidly the lion might break his teeth on him, while still another, getting the full implications of the situation as his feelings rush upon him, very gently but efficiently reaches for his gun and shoots the animal. Only in the last case did the man use the emotions. In the other cases the persons were completely dominated by their emotions – either negatively, completely withdrawing from reality, or positively, taking a rash and quite unwarranted action. The proper use of the emotions enables one to see and understand a situation as it really is, make the right judgment, and so meet the situation wisely.

Something happens which one sees, hears or senses in some way. One reacts. One feels anxious, elated, threatened, depressed, resentful, angry, disgusted, sad, pleased, joyful, hopeful, encouraged, and so on. Man experiences, or ought to experience, a full spectrum of emotions or reactions to each life situation, according to its nature. None of these feelings is in itself good or bad. It is merely important that it get through, register correctly, present the right information. The earlier and more clearly the message comes through, the more time and calm is provided for working out the right decision and the appropriate action.

The teacher, for example, depends to an extreme on her properly operating emotions, for the handling of her class. Children quite typically take the measure of the teacher, very early – will she run them or will they run her? A child sets out to challenge the teacher, to irritate her. Made aware of the challenge, the teacher reacts with a slow burn (called burn because it is felt), she gets hot under the collar. This reaction, amber light, tips her off to the direction of her reaction to the happening, that she is verging on anger. The warning leads her to handle the situation correctly for the best interest of the child, the class, and her own poise and effectiveness. She has the power to cool it, to simmer down. She needs no more reaction; she got the message. What is required now is thought – how to handle the situation? She uses her wisdom and experience to avoid lashing out at the child, which would be precipitate, unfair, probably both unhappy and wasted. Her overreaction would only set off another, there would be a complete impasse and polarization of sympathies, an unnecessary confrontation. The good teacher's emotions are recognized and used long before they reach hurricane force. They serve their purpose well by prodding the mind to provide a prudent and wise solution to the problem presented. Teachers who overreact, and those who allow themselves to be threatened or intimidated, are all emotionally dominated, and can only handle such situations badly.

There is no choice connected with the emotions, no freedom. They are mechanical, automatic, infallible indicators of the situation presenting itself for management. The emotions cannot tell lies, but they can be interfered with by the master power of the person, who can suppress them or insist on taking the wrong message from them. However, their abuse is always a mistake. Every emotion is a very identifiable feeling with its proper name, expressing a specific, normal reaction to a situation to which it points as surely as a compass needle. If read correctly, it indicates the nature of the situation with which one is presented. The rule for the emotions is: never suppress them, never exploit them, always express them; that is, permit them to be felt, so that they can be recognized and used in the relationships one must have with other people and other things. Everyone else does not have to know how I feel, but I must know, so that I can be aware of the situation as it truly is, and so make judgments about it as demanded by truth and love.

Many people handle their emotions badly because it has been all but accepted over the years that the emotions were the problem rather than infallible indicators of the solution. When someone was described as "emotional" it seemed more an accusation than a statement of fact.

Man is essentially emotional and would be hopelessly handicapped otherwise. Unfortunately the term was applied to those who vented their emotions on others, abused them rather than used them for their own insight and personal understanding. It was a social sin to express one's emotions and a virtue to suppress them in the name of the famous "stiff upper lip" of good behaviour. Those who think of emotions as bad, or accept the stupidity that "one must rise above one's feelings" by suppressing them, actually never allow these feelings to register, and so have to be out of touch with the true situations around themselves. The emotional reactions of such people often register on those standing around them, without being felt by the persons whose emotions they are. Those who suppress their feelings are bland, colourless, and deep-frozen to protect themselves from pain, even the most necessary and helpful. People who exploit their emotions, that is, wallow in them and are carried away by them, are social menaces and incapable of relating to others in a responsible way.

The clear messages of the emotions are always rejected by people for whom the truth is bad news. They cannot or will not face real situations, and the rejected messages from their emotions usually result in various psychosomatic illnesses. When permitted to dominate, positively or negatively, abused emotions can lead to addictions of every kind, to tension, confusion and such depression that there is often complete inability to cope with even the minor realities of life. The alcoholic, for whom the bottle is bigger than the man, the fat slob addicted to the refrigerator, trying vainly to fill an empty life with food, the drug addict whose idea of "precious" is the little pill or the hypodermic needle which carries him to the never-never land, the sex addict for whom copulation is love, are all emotional cop-outs.

Certainly, real human relationships of any kind are beyond the emotionally suppressed, unfeeling person. Obviously a healthy emotional life is vital for anyone hoping to achieve a true loving relationship. Since emotions are the inner eyes of man, it is hard to understand why one who does not despise his eyes could be disdainful or frightened of his feelings. It is silly for a man to refuse pain however useful or necessary, or to embrace pleasure however harmful or destructive, but that is precisely what is done when the emotions are ignored or mismanaged. The depressed person will register nothing which is happy or joyful, the elated person will register nothing which burdens or obligates.

The high incidence of emotional illness today is due both to better understanding (and so greater fear of the havoc wrought by abuse of the emotions) and the vastly increased emotional pressure of current living, and the inability of people to meet that pressure. In times past there was much more general tranquillity and a much slower pace to life. Healthy emotions today must be like highly sensitive radar. A few years ago the eyes and the foghorns were enough to take care of ships in the fog. Ships were fewer, travelled more slowly, and were so constructed as to give without disintegrating on impact. However in the space age there are new requirements. A keener eye is needed to sense objects through fog and in darkness. Radar was cleverly invented and devised, a supersensitivity to what could not be seen. The naked eye cannot directly handle air traffic, even on the clearest day, when hundreds of huge craft hurtling through space depend on human judgment to land and take off without accident. The more sensitive the radar the more time and wider margin for safe decision is possible. The emotions are the radar of human behaviour and now need to be more sensitive than ever to make right judgment possible in the complicated human relations of modern society.

The emotions must be seen as tremendous assets, never as liabilities. The higher the evaluation of them, the more quickly and gladly is recognized the role they must play and their tragic mismanagement will be much less. Through their wizard use the successful salesman sizes up his prospect with real insight and tailors his pitch to him. The same correct use of them is equally effective in all human relationships. Through them comes the insight to appreciate the positions of others, to understand and compassionate them, to know a friend from an enemy, to cement the bond of friendship and reconcile oneself to an enemy. They enable a man to handle himself well in most situations and to bring harmony from most discords. Nowhere are they more vital than in loving. Through reading them correctly true values are discovered in the loved one, understanding is made possible, and love endures. It is the emotions which double a joy and halve a sorrow shared. It is through them that one approaches his friends in love in the first place. They are indispensable both in the approach to long-lasting, loving relationships and wise and happy marriages, and in avoiding seduction through impossible relationships with incompatible people. The emotions, badly understood and miserably managed, have broken up more possible love relationships, more meetings of minds and councils of the wise than most other factors. Handled well, they give the feel of coming events and usher them gently into the arena of reason where they are worked out satisfactorily.

The dictionary's use of the words "think" and "feel" interchangeably reflects very well the tendency of the emotions to usurp by default the place and work of the mind. Although the emotional centres are in the brain, the emotions must never be confused with the mind. Their functions are poles apart, though the emotions are handmaid to the mind. It is a mistake to identify what one feels about something with what one thinks about it. All knowledge coming through the senses is filtered through the emotions to the cerebral cortex which does the computing, the thinking. The rampant emotions play havoc with the data processing of the mind: the deep-frozen emotions, which do not process information, deprive the mind of the material for its work.

When the mind, whose object is the truth, betrays its trust, as it does when it rationalizes invalid foregone conclusions, it rejects the painful truth or accepts the pleasant lie by suppressing or exploiting the emotions, which normally express the situation to the mind as it really is. Nothing so impedes the pursuit of truth as the blocking of the emotions' automatic message. The best of minds do not work well when correct data does not reach them, as in the case of the emotionally disturbed or ill, who cannot differentiate between their emotions and their minds, between what they feel and what they think.

The emotions must not be confused with conscience, which is a moral judgment about the goodness or the badness of something thought, said or done. There are no feelings directly connected with conscience. There is a tremendous tendency in good people to believe they are guilty when they feel guilty, while many evil people feel very little if any guilt. There is a great difference between guilt feelings before and after the fact of wrongdoing. The anxiety of many good people to do right, so akin to the fear of wrongdoing, is often interpreted by them as an indication of wrongdoing or guilt. Guilt feelings, so closely related to anxiety and often identified with it, come in anticipation of doing anything contrary to accepted pattern, even when the pattern was set by ignorance, or by tyrannical authority wielded unjustly or dishonestly. Innocent people often feel anxious, and/or guilty, when stopped for any reason by a policeman. Those reared in authoritarian families, or trained under authority-obedience-oriented regimes, tend to concede guilt in the face of censorious authority, to meekly accept misunderstanding, to abdicate their right to question and, sometimes, even their freedom. They do not "feel" equality in the presence of a uniform or have an awareness of their personal dignity or rights in the presence of authority. Such guilt feelings in the innocent, and the reaction to them by the good, have permitted evil to be done in

he name of God and under the guise of good. Good people, faced with
authority, too seldom ask the right questions or demand justice or a
course of action worthy of God or of the power authority lays claim to.

True guilt feelings, like all the feelings, are very helpful and worthwhile. They are the best possible warning in the face of a situation
requiring deeper thought and further consideration, before something is
done hastily or irresponsibly. Acting much as the emotion of genuine
anxiety does, they create sincere concern and disposition for a second
good hard look before action follows. Guilt feelings after wrongdoing,
of course, dispose one to regret, remorse and restitution, because they
are so hard to live with. Hardened criminals have inured themselves so
well to such feelings that they hardly register unless the code of thieves
itself is broken. In such cases it is more fear than guilt that alerts them
to what is done and the price to be paid if they are caught. The
"worst" feelings do not make one bad, any more than the "best"
feelings make one good. The feelings of a man never make him guilty;
that comes from what he is and does, from full malice aforethought.

The emotions must not be confused with gross selfishness. Emotionally dominated people do things which are commonly misinterpreted as
selfish, mainly because they cannot escape the compulsion of their
feelings. That others are involved in what they do or want hardly
crosses the threshhold of their consciousness. Pleasure is irresistible to
them and pain is unacceptable. They are always undisciplined. The
genuinely selfish person, on the other hand, is neither immature nor
irresponsible. He knows what should be done and is quite capable of
doing it but simply refuses to do it, chooses not to do it because it does
not suit him. He lacks virtue and generally is vicious, but he is
disciplined.

People who are uncomfortable when they are enjoying themselves,
because of their fear of doing wrong, are also emotional cripples. God
did not put an unqualified curse on pleasure nor an unqualified blessing
on pain. Many "good" people find a strange comfort in pain and
suffering, which they consider a mark of distinction, and even enjoy.
The emotional health of such people leaves much to be desired. They
are not at all like the emotionally mature people whose ability to
accept unavoidable pain and suffering does keep pain within its very
real limitations.

In picking out one set or category of emotions one must remember
its relationship to the others, otherwise it is like discussing one key or
note on the piano without reference to the instrument or to piano

music. The sexual emotions cannot be isolated and understood without reference to all the emotions. But everything said about the emotions in general also applies to the sexual emotions.

Since man is by nature sexual, he must feel sexual. He is born with genitals which he must feel strongly inclined to use. There is something wrong with the person who does not feel that inclination. However there is a tremendous tendency to stress only the genital aspect of the sexual emotions. But the basic indication of normal sexual emotions is the very real need a man feels for a woman and a woman for a man, not only as a companion in copulation but as a personal companion, helpmate, confidant and lover. Male and female complement each other personally as well as sexually. When this mutual need is either suppressed or exploited, the result has to be poor intersexual relationships. People normally respond sexually to a sexual stimulus, and everyone of the opposite sex is a sexual stimulus. All other things being equal (and in practice they never are), there should be a greater interest and rapport between man and woman than between two of the same sex.

The sexual emotions can be discussed, but not understood, out of context with the sexual mores and customs of the period. People do not change but customs do. Our grandmothers would have *felt*, and been considered, quite naked in a bathing suit modest by today's standards. Modern openness has removed the taboo from the subjects of sex and sexuality so that they can be discussed now with more detachment than some other bodily functions. In actual fact, in our society, there is year-round open season for sex. There is no way that anyone can dispense himself from a personal confrontation with sex and the proper management of its related emotions. An urgent study and understanding of this matter is inescapable and vital if one is to cope with modern living. The wisdom and virtue required to manage in it come only from easy familiarity with the sexual emotions and full acceptance of one's own sexuality.

The inexperienced and undisciplined have little or no defence against their sex emotions gone wild, or the encouragement, so prevalent in our society, to exploit them. Not only is sex ridiculously considered sufficient basis for a long-term relationship, but it is widely accepted as a functional need as indispensable as eating or breathing. Many people tend to comfort themselves in these distortions of truth with a homemade conscience formed almost entirely by how they *feel*. So, too many are carried headlong into marriages they *feel* to be right because they are *in love* rather than because they love deeply and well. Lured or compelled by sex, they often eagerly burden themselves prematurely with marriage, a serious obligation they are incapable of handling, and subsequently with children they are ill equipped to raise. The children of such marriages are often conceived unwanted and gestated resentfully, and considered intruders who are denied the mature love of happy parents. They are destined to become emotional cripples, to join the protest march through life of the innumerable unloved, to make a mockery of marriage and to stand as evidence of the rarity of real love.

The sexual emotions are strong but, like all the other emotions, they are far from irresistible. They are certainly less strong than anger or fear, to say nothing of insecurity. But until they are well understood, they will continue unresisted to dominate the followers of the pied piper of sexual permissiveness. The sex-dominated person is as emoionally immature as any other emotion-dominated person, and functions beneath the level of reason, as a child, not so much immorally as emotionally.

How then do the sexual emotions work ? How can emotional health be gauged from the sexual point of view ?

The sex emotions do not really make themselves consciously felt until puberty. Infants do have genital awareness. Infant males do have erections and females do respond in an infantile way to sexual stimuli, but these reactions are about as purely physical as feelings can be. Such sexual awareness is on a very basic plane of consciousness. These experiences do have a very minimal emotional effect, but nothing like the effect of the emotions specifically dealt with, or avoided, on a highly conscious level. They are more physical than personal experiences, with more superficial than deep or lasting effects. They dispose, rather than compel, children towards emotional problems.

There is incontrovertible evidence of the incredible influence of the first year of life on emotional conditioning, growth and development. Infants and children require the security of a love-oriented milieu in which to experience their emotions and so gradually learn how to integrate them into real living. The emotional state of most disturbed people is correctly traced back to their childhood environment and reflects their few happy experiences, and the many unfortunate ones that inhibit their eager acceptance and promote the frightened uncertainty characterizing their emotional lives. During the childhood years there is ample opportunity to experience, and accept, the emotions in the protective atmosphere of a loving home where they can be contended with under minimal pressure. If a healthy pattern of emotional living is well begun before the severe pressure of the sexual emotions is experienced, this pattern will minimize the impact of the sexual emotions and reduce the chances of disastrous consequences of the trial and error learning process. The way the sexual emotions will be handled is determined almost completely by the way the other emotions have been met and handled prior to puberty. The emotionally healthy child moves into adolescence and adult sexual life with the assurance carried forward from prior successful emotional experience. He adjusts to sex without being dominated by his sexual feelings or fear of them. Fully accepting his sexuality, he integrates it comfortably into his loving.

The growth of children towards conscious sexuality, therefore, depends greatly on their general emotional health. Emotionally indulged children, those reared in general permissiveness, will be victims of their sex emotions, which they exploit freely for all available pleasure or suppress only to avoid possible pain. They find discipline intolerable and are in deep emotional trouble before they have any appreciable awareness of the damage being done. The problem of the overdisciplined child is as acute; prissiness, disdain for sex, snobbery and a false set of standards are not healthy signs. But the overdisciplined child, aided by the normal pull of healthy sex emotions, has a far better chance of adjusting downward to a healthy attitude than has the indulged adolescent of adjusting upward to discipline. The latter finds it nearly impossible to achieve the discipline for minimal order in his life. The course to health for the emotional slob is much more difficult than that from rigid discipline, though neither inflexibility nor flaccidity is ever a virtue.

The child of temper tantrums and sulks predictably mishandles his sexual emotions, as does the victim of unfortunate and frightening sexual childhood experience. This is likewise true of those threatened with dire moral consequences of sexual acts nearly meaningless to the child but given undue seriousness by frightened adults hypersensitive to sexual experience. Childhood discoveries, experiments and experiences must never be given a moral significance which only adult crimes could have. Young people should be adequately instructed in the normal manifestations of the sexual emotions which have nothing directly to do with morals or propriety. Certainly, the mechanical stimulation of his own newly discovered genitals by the experimenting child has none of the formal, but only the material, qualities of wrongness. Moral significance must be based on understanding and the willingness to do known evil. While masturbation often has no more moral significance for the child than a temper tantrum, because of the ignorance or secrecy usually surrounding sex the problem is not dealt with as directly or ably as are temper tantrums. When the problem is faced squarely, without preconceived notions, the stupidity of deliberate masturbation is easily established and ultimately avoided. The common occurrence of masturbation does not make it desirable, much less commendable, as many counselors would have it. Even though it may be less harmful than other conditions it is still an emotional setback or failure. It reveals an exploitative tendency which is a real obstacle to the genuine outgoingness of love. It is a turning in on oneself for a pleasure not experienced outside, either through rejection, fear of rejection, or a sense of personal inadequacy. The pleasure content of masturbation is as limited as that of any feeling. Only the person who misguidedly makes any pleasure, however harmful, a good thing in itself, can recommend masturbation.

It is normal, and to be expected, that the first conscious awareness of the specifically sexual emotions, that is the venereal and very pleasurable feelings experienced in the genital areas of the body, will jolt and disturb. There is the novelty and high excitement of discovery, and an unusually intense preoccupation for a considerable time with this specific and sometimes apparently isolated function, which can be enlightening and healthy or to an equal degree morbid and unhealthy. This is a time for which early sex education should prepare the child. Parents should be equipped and ready to understand it and to help to the necessary and desirable degree. However, it is to be expected that the emotionally healthy child will move into it quite naturally and should not need extraordinary help. He is alarmed and upset by apprehensive parents who project their own sexual hangups, or incompetent teachers with morbid sexual fascination. No child is ready for the sexual discovery unless he has experienced love sufficiently to sense intuitively that the human sexual act is related to loving, that it must be purposeful and tied into the over-all interests and welfare of the human person. The dignity and worthiness of human sex is part of this concept.

The purely physical aspect of sex dominates early awareness. It is far more related to self than to others. It always has moral overtones regardless of the pearls of wisdom of modern psychology or the

Olympian platitudes of social philosophers to the contrary. Puberty is the expressed peak of self-awareness, intriguingly novel and somewhat overwhelming in its accompanying feelings of independence and defiance. It is the first sense of being an island in the sea of humanity, and lonely and lost in being so. There is a feeling of asocialness and of kicking off the burnt-out first-stage rocket of childhood, of being half man and half boy, of spurning yet still needing a mother. There is a vague awareness of a self-assertiveness made possible by a continuing protectiveness of home and family, the beginning of self-determination and self-sufficiency. The adolescent still retains most of the privileges without having assumed any of the more serious social obligations. He is at his freest, entering adulthood without being an adult. He is reacting sexually with a power not previously experienced. He wants to make himself, and his presence, felt. Before this, long before this, he should have learned from those around him that a well-ordered emotional life is essential to successful and happy living in the relationships he has with others. If this truth has been assimilated, one has sufficient emotional health, even at an early age, for either the celibate state of loving or a realistic marriage. Youthful marriages or youthful vocations are usually failures only because of emotional immaturity.

Sexual reactions occasion a serious and more profound attention to others. One's awareness is more acute, his desire to relate more specific, genitally directed. Here his early emotional experience manifests itself. If his experience with the outside world to which he reached eagerly and uninhibited as a child was unfortunate, he will tend to withdraw defensively, turn in on himself, become a loner. If he met indulgence and grew up uncontrolled, using his other emotions to expoloit others, he will tend to exploit sexually those who attract him or awaken his sexual desires. However, if he is emotionally healthy his sexual relations will be accepted in the larger context of love; he will not misunderstand them. Whenever he reacts sexually, knowing that he relates whole person to whole person, the accompanying emotions of tenderness and personal interest will not be lost on him, but will keep him love-aware as well as sex-aware. His sexual emotions will be invaluable to him as the starting point towards personal love. They will present him with the strongest impetus to relate to another person intimately, to share himself with another in a way hitherto unexperienced. He will not permit fear to choke off the accompanying emotions of tenderness, concern, generosity and self-sacrifice. The sexual emotions will stimulate him to a giving and a responsibility which simply will not develop unless he understands sex correctly and integrates it into his loving. This precise experience of the sexual emotions, not merely experienced but understood, more than any other is the emotional contribution to the making of a real man or woman.

At the time of the first full bloom of the sexual emotions, it is important to be sensitive enough to receive their message at the earliest possible moment and correctly. It is not an accident that the increased sensitivity of pubescence is noticeable by almost anyone. But, unfortunately, though this high sensitivity is generally admitted, it is seldom appreciated. It is the tragedy of puberty that many do not recognize the thrust of their sexual emotions until they have reached such a pitch as to carry all before them. This can be the death of love, simply because tragic experience does not inspire one to try again to find real love. The ill-considered action, precipitated by sexual excitement, too easily deludes the young about the degree of personal relationship involved. It is virtually impossible to tell people *in love* that they do not know each other well or that their relationship is based purely on superficialities. Most people simply do not try, hoping that the structure of such relationships will crash under the weight of its own emotional content. Unfortunately the emotionally dominated acquire little wisdom and even consider their own minds antagonistic to the felt needs which dominate them. If the mind has been trained from childhood to recognize the merit of truth, its real object, and to recognize in the emotions invaluable faculties of precise, if limited, competence, reporting validly only the *felt* situation, there is some hope that the limitations of the sex emotions will not only be understood but accepted. The best the emotions can reveal is the feeling *now*, present tense, about anyone. The emotions are so limited to the present that people who live by their feelings can contradict themselves from day to day, without being liars, simply because they feel differently about things when a little time has elapsed. This is nowhere truer than of the sexual emotions. They are quite incapable of expressing a personal relationship which is a matter of mind and will, past, present and future, and the many qualities in both people which are essential to a deep loving relationship. All they can do is report a localized feeling at the moment.

Greater appreciation of the sexual emotions assures better relating to others. Every genital feeling is a sexual emotion pure and simple. It expresses infallibly nothing more or less than a need, a genital interest in, and attraction to, one of the opposite sex. However, it is at times the dominant feeling, but it should never be permitted either through ignorance or default to block out the myriad other feelings relating to a person or an object. One can develop awareness of these other feelings, which, though present, are not strong enough to make their presence felt in the sexually dominated. Each of these other feelings has a message of its own. If felt and read correctly, they make a multidimensional situation clear. They save one from domination by a single emotion and an unreal, one-dimensional pursuit – for example, the man in bed with another's wife who in the heat of passion does not even notice the husband enter the room with a gun. Other emotional stars in the sexual galaxy are tenderness, concern, protectiveness, anxiety, the joy and elation of friendly companionship and sharing, the delight of discovery of the new world of another person. These messages from the emotions, in the mature person, get just as much of a hearing as the genital ones, which may be louder but are no more meaningful. When they get that hearing, they take the rough edges and urgency away from the genital sexual emotions and present sex in the context of personal relationship and responsibility. In one who appreciates the truth, getting these messages insures the relationship against the dead end of sexploitation.

The sexual emotions can never, on their own, drive one to sexual indulgence. In this regard the sexual emotions have been given a very bad name, which they do not deserve. They dominate only when permitted, or encouraged, to do so. Rather than being accepted as simple emotions, they are considered a roaring lion waiting to devour the unwary. They are endowed with a ferocity and irresistibility which no emotion naturally has. They seem to tyrannize the undisciplined and indulgent only because they fill the vacuum left in these persons by unthinkingness and weakness of will. Quite the contrary to tyrannizing, the sexual emotions make themselves felt early enough to assure their direction to a genuine relationship by anyone understanding and esteeming love for the tremendous achievement that it is. They are not toys to be played with but faculties to be employed in the interest of the whole person. Like all emotions, they call to judgment – in this instance about the place of sex in the relationship presented. They strongly suggest the management of sex rather than its domination. They make the use of sex by love possible. It is quite true that sexually dominated or fearful, sexually suppressed people, erroneously convinced that sex is bigger than the man, cannot afford the luxury of sexually stimulating situations because they will perish in them. However this is not the fault of the sexual emotions aroused in the situations but a result of the emotional ill health of the people involved, who cannot use their feelings well.

The healthy man gladly receives the information from his sexual emotions because he knows that no one need at any time be dominated by any emotion. He knows that sex is not more difficult to handle than anger, jealousy or elation. The healthy man feels adequate as a person, is convinced of his manhood and general normalcy. He can handle his emotions.

Manhood, to the emotionally, sexually controlled man, is the ability to love rather than the compulsion to copulate. The sexual emotions do not frighten or panic him, nor does he engage in the silly business of deluding himself about his control by playing one emotion against another as fearful or jealous people do. His well used sexual emotions switch on his cerebral cortex which evaluates the relationship at hand and sets a course for its successful development, or orders it aborted. Far from leading one into temptation, the sexual emotions can preserve one from it. They cannot pretend to be something they are not; they are never the basis, but merely the occasion, of love. They never manage to throw the intelligence of the mature person out of gear.

The Judeo-Christian heritage of sexual teachings and taboos, the litany of Western man's unfortunate experiences with himself and his relationships in his journey through history, caused the sexual emotions to be looked upon with a jaundiced eye. It became a virtue to suppresss the sexual emotions by invoking fear, an even stronger emotion. Fear was the scalpel used in the psychological surgery by which sex was removed, in the delusion that chastity was possible without sex emotions. The chronic state of fear brought on sexual inadequacy; and the use of fear left people morally defenceless in situations in which they were not afraid. Much like those who avoided copulation for fear of V.D. until penicillin was discovered, or for fear of pregnancy before the Pill, there was nothing to save them from themselves when the fear of sex was removed. They then were sexually dominated as they had been fear-dominated.

Undue fear of sex drilled into young people to "protect" them from themselves not only deprives them of the occasions required for the practice of chastity, but also of the opportunity to learn to love in preparation for marriage or celibacy. Nervous confessors, projecting their own fears, have made a virtue – erroneously called prudence, sometimes chastity – of young people's withdrawing from sexual and loving situations. Yet they can never learn to love well in any other situations. The toll of premarital unloving is obvious everywhere in the incredible number of unhappy Christian marriages. Too many young people were encouraged to believe that love would come to them automatically through the sacraments, or in some mysterious way other than the school of painfully acquired discipline and the power to act well in loving situations. Where the sexual emotions are not experienced there is no occasion for chastity, which is the power to act lovingly under the pressure of the sexual emotions. Certainly, man is not improved by replacing cultural and religious taboos with contraceptives and abortions rather than virtue and understanding. Apart from the fact that these substitutes leave him with little self-respect, they are the stuff of which emotional cripples are made – line-of-least-resistance, head-in-the-sand solutions temporizing with reality.

A common consequence of mismanagement of the sexual emotions is continual suspicion of the sexual involvement of others. Since emotionally sick people believe sex is bigger than they are, and judge others by themselves, what else could they believe about men and women associating together? They are fascinated by gossip and scandal of a sexual nature on which they feed their own suppressed and often unconscious sexual appetites. This characteristic is plainly manifest in the insatiable appetites of perfectly "nice" people for the dirty novel with little or no redeeming literary merit, reviewed and praised by commercial hacks whose acclaim gives some aura of respectability to reading it. The healthy acceptance of, and ability to love with, normal sexual feelings makes sexual fantasy or furtive vicarious sex experience a superfluous bore.

The sexual arousal, so purposeful and desirable at specific and chosen times in loving marriage, need not take place in the loving of unmarried people who understand that love is much greater and broader than sex. In the loving situation they will not be carried away by their sexual emotions if they have the same basic understanding and control of their sexual appetites as the patient, peaceful man has of his temper. All people who, despite their inclinations to the contrary, elect to do what is best have such emotional control. When man makes sex an end in itself he is claiming the genital pleasure from the mechanical function of the sex organs as high human achievement, which it is not. If it were, one could not question the emotional health or stability of people in seemingly stable marriages who suddenly find themselves in love with a stranger and desert their husbands or wives and children, or whom they feel little love. These people do not understand what the human achievement of love is or the virtue and discipline which strengthen it.

The old spiritual writers pointed out the close relationship between patience and chastity. The common factor they observed was that the impatient and the unchaste man was easily aroused, emotionally dominated, lacked the power and discipline to use his emotions to occasion the practice of virtue, which, of course, is the meaning of emotional health. The sexual emotions have much to contribute to that emotional health which makes it possible to achieve love. Love is the prize of the patient, understanding person, rather than of the capricious, easily aroused one.

CHAPTER SIX

The Spirituality of Sex

Man's constant preoccupation, from the beginning of time, with the concept of a Supreme Being is evidence of the spiritual dimension in man. His power to believe in his fellow man whom he loves, as well as God, is again evidence of the spiritual dimension by which man contends with the things he does not know or only partially understands. This spiritual dimension is where man establishes his hierarchy of values, weighs the good and evil of his actions and makes the judgments which he calls conscience. It is the arena in which he measures his motives and contends with the imponderables of human life, where he faces the fact that he must take credit or blame for all things he thinks, says and does, which have a special significance because they are neither automatic nor inconsequential things, but human actions. In his spiritual dimension he confronts the truth and measures his actions by it: there he assents in belief and demands action on what he believes. There he decides what love is, and then loves truly and well. In the spiritual dimension man receives life's charter from God, his potential to be a thinking, loving, sexual person. The spiritual dimension is the locale of the interpersonal relationship called love.

It is in his spiritual life that man integrates sex into the spiritual experience of loving. There he comes to grips with the truth about sex, sees himself honestly in his failures. There he experiences the strong urge to be good, to be better, to love. The redemptive power of love makes itself felt in the spiritual dimension and inspires him to repent, to change for the better, to grow personally. Those who reject the spiritual dimension identify happiness with pleasure and therefore never know happiness, for pleasure as an end in itself simply does not work. Nothing is pure pleasure. Pleasure is essentially a quality of experience lived in the context of a whole life, and is helpful or harmful in so far as it contributes to or detracts from that life. Man can plainly see that his life aches with loneliness as much as his stomach aches from hunger. His minds thirsts for the spiritual as his body craves fluids. His mind and his will love as naturally as his body copulates. By nature he is a creature of the spiritual and the material worlds, equally at home in either, fully at home in neither.

The mediaeval philosophers speculated about the number of angels meeting on the point of a needle. Inflated scientists missed the point. The philosophers pondered, and tried to understand, the union of spirit and matter which they plainly saw to be a fact in man. The Latin word for spirit, soul or psyche is *anima*, which means life, animation. They wanted to know how a spiritual substance like the soul actually moved the physical body: why unhappiness could make people physically ill. Once, most diseases were considered to be purely physical but now man knows better and accepts the psychosomatic element in all his illnesses. Emotionally based illness illustrates particularly well the inseparable relationship of the spirit (psyche) to the body (soma), as man's unhappiness with himself, his conflicts and his inability to love are reflected in his body's physical malfunction.

The philosophers also knew there was a real connection between a man's genitals and his mind, his spirit. The spiritual life of man in apposition to sexual life is the life of God and grace in the human soul. But the sexual life of man essentially involves God and grace in that life and goes into the making of everything that man is, so it must add to or detract from his role as a person. Man's peace of mind, his happiness, relates directly to his harmonious sexual relations, since his sexual life is as essentially spiritual as he is. To speak of man as an angel is as ridiculous as to speak of him as a beast. Any effort to rise above sex like an angel, or copulate unthinkingly like a beast, distorts man's humanity. He may copulate piggishly, stupidly, criminally, or happily, lovingly, generously, but he always does so as a man, a human being. His basest actions have some spiritual significance because they are always reasoned or willed to some small degree, no matter how subconsciously or unwisely. Because man's sexual life always involves the choice of functioning or not functioning, it cannot be categorized as a bowel movement, as pseudo-scientists would have it. Human copulation is a matter of choice; nothing can compel a person so to function if unwilling, or restrain him if he wishes (external force left aside, of course).

The man without an arm or leg is obviously not whole; the unfeeling person is plainly not all there. Man without his spiritual dimension lacks integrity as a person. It is wrong to insist that the more spiritual a man is the less carnal he should be, for man is spirit incarnate, soul in flesh. Both his spirituality and sexuality peak in loving. Thus celibates fail when they get too bogged down in their spirituality to love; married people fail when they get too bogged down in their sexual life to love. When sexual life is exaggerated to the detriment of the spiritual, people are unable to move through sex to personal loving. When sex becomes so formidable to celibates that they cannot accept the fact of it in loving, they become fear-dominated, withdrawn, generally suspicious, frustrated people. Married spirituality peaks when sexual intercourse is so happily integrated into the loving life that it does not distract husband or wife from their personal union, but in fact contributes to it. The time, manner and frequency of sexual intercourse is determined by love in those marriages in which spiritual values dominate, in which the personal union is deepest and most rewarding.

Sex is a matter of spiritual concern simply because it is a function worthy of man, a thoroughly human function. For this reason sex can never be simply a matter of technique or finesse but is always a vital personal matter. The spirituality of sex may be understood more clearly by considering the human hand. What is its meaning in itself and its function? One appreciates its value best by being deprived of it, for it has little value apart from the person whose hand it is. Everything that it does well or badly adds to or detracts from the person. The person can never repudiate the actions of his hand, or disclaim responsibility for what it does as if the action did not come from his mind, or the motives and meaning of the action derive from the set of values dominating his life. Certainly the hand which reaches for the privilege but rejects the obligation serves the person badly. Can less be said of the genitals?

Historically, sexual orgies have often played a major role in superstitious religious worship. To get away from this "pagan abomination", Christianity tended to downgrade sex without considering such action censorious of God, who created sex. It followed from this that chastity soon outranked charity in importance, and on this basis celibate life was given a significance high above the married state without due consideration of the degree of the loving of the people involved. Sexlessness, rather than love, became the measure of holiness, and frigidity and coldness were accepted as purity and detachment. They are, in fact, sure signs of spiritual immaturity and indicate a fear-dominated, inadequate person who cannot accept sex as worthy of man, or understand love. Anyone incapable of a good sexual performance is rarely if ever loving. Since such a one usually finds sex degrading, even bestial, he escapes it in a pseudospirituality buttressed by high, but false, motives. This mentality dismisses the beauty of the Song of Solomon as embarrassing. There, sensual human love is used to depict the relationship of God to the soul, in terms very understandable to the man of the times. The blushing puritan is offended by the use of such terms to describe God's purely spiritual love. While God's love for man is purely spiritual, as befits His nature, man's love for God, however spiritual, can be experienced only in the way of a male or female, as befits human nature.

Man's penchant for judging others by himself is extended even to God, whom man understandably tends to cast in his own image and likeness. It seems logical, however ridiculous, to believe that if man is a little like God then God must be a little like man. It is one thing to appreciate the inadequacy of the anthropomorphic God, another to reject God because of the inadequacy of man's understanding and terminology. It is in this vein that the command not to commit adultery seems like a censure of sex rather than God's marvellous way of telling man that his sexual fulfilment will be found only in the permanent commitment of a loving marriage where man's interest is in the person rather than the mere function. "Thou shalt not commit adultery" casts no aspersions on sex, which was God's idea in the first place. Nor is it God's way of taking the fun out of life. It merely insists that sex in the life of man is not the same as sex in the lives of the beasts. It is simply that man's personal happiness and fulfilment are possible only in the restriction of sexual intercourse to a person to whom he dedicates himself wholly for life. Coitus is a thing to be done only by the deeply loving man or woman. Taken out of this context, sex can have as little significance as a bowel movement. Man is made to have sexual intercourse, not as a well functioning set of genitals but as a spiritual being performing a very meaningful human act. Love lifts the act from a context of mere pleasure to a state of happiness deriving from the relationship of the people. The place of sex in human love becomes a fact, experience, in the spiritual dimension of man.

To make sex an end in itself is to remove it from loving, to lower man's centre of gravity from his person to his sensory faculties. Man's spirituality, which integrates sex into loving, leads him into the loving union with God in heaven where sex has no place, simply because it could add nothing to the intensity of the personal union with God and others there. The spiritualization of genital sex makes man aware that his sexual life is inseparable from his loving life, and that its role is to contribute to the personal fulfilment of loving. Genital sex pleasure is mistaken for the "best there is" only by those who have not achieved the happiness of loving. The spiritual man integrates his sex into loving rather than his love into sex, as most would have it. The spiritual man also accepts that his genital, procreative function is not merely something to be played with, because in it he shares in a special way the very creativity of God.

It is precisely the man with a healthy spiritual life who can relinquish life itself, let alone its attractive pleasures, for a principle in which he believes, or for a fellow man he loves. He has the virtue, that is, the power to do what ought to be done, in sexual matters, as in all things involved in personal fulfilment. He can engage in or refrain from sexual intercourse simply because he loves. Man's sex life can be dominated by many factors, but it is when those factors are standards beyond the material, a true set of values, that sex does contribute to the happiness of the person. Under the spiritual influence of love, sexual intercourse is purposefully performed with real happiness and joy.

Scientific studies of sexual intercourse lose their validity primarily because they discount, or ignore entirely, the spiritual dimension essentially present in all human behaviour, being content to investigate sex on a purely mechanistic or technical basis isolated from all that a man is. Regardless of his feelings, man simply cannot slough off the spiritual significance of his sexual life. His earthiest actions are dominated by a hierarchy of values which, to be genuine, must represent the world of the spirit. Hungry men can fast for a worthy cause as married people or celibates can refrain from sexual intercourse for a reason. Surely to be of loving service to the people of God is ample reason for celibates to refrain from sexual intercourse for life.

Man's children can be born through love, lust or indifference, by design or by accident. Man can get rid of undesirables by abortion or breed bodies to supply organ transplants for privileged or important citizens. But whatever he chooses to do, he cannot escape the consequences of his actions nor repudiate the world of his options. It is absolutely ridiculous to think that the use of his genitals can rightly be capricious or irresponsible, or dominated by his feelings of the moment, completely out of the context of reality. Unless the genitals are used in conformity with a set of standards including the spiritual motivations and sanctions open to him, values which are moral as well as material, the result will inevitably be personally and socially monstrous. It is surely reasonable to consider that man is made to do his own thing, but that thing is what he is made for rather than merely what he feels at the moment.

It is thoroughly regrettable that the expression "to turn on" is generally restricted to emotional excitement. It describes beautifully the spiritual power of the loving person to enkindle others, brighten their lives, evoke warm tenderness and deep love. The spiritual dimension's relationship to sex consists in its power to direct sex into acute awareness of others and active interest in them, not as bodies but as people. Surely the union of two people in a common, worthy cause is much deeper, more fully human than the union of a man and woman in the exclusively sexual embrace. It is a fundamental frustration of marriage that the sexual embrace in itself does not bring the people, but merely the bodies, closer. Love and understanding unite people more closely than sex ever can. Yet only God and man have a deeper union than the husband and wife whose sexual embrace is but the beginning of a personal intermingling far surpassing the actual limitations of pure sex.

Sexual reactions to people are normal steps in the discovery of personal beauty, truth and goodness, things deeply esteemed because of the spiritual dimension. If a consequent relationship involves the total sexual giving to each other in love, it is because the person-to-person interest, understanding and love made it possible. Lacking spiritual depth and high human values, many naively see a meaning and promise in the precipitate sexual adventure which is not really there. Such an eventuality is avoided by sufficient spiritualization of sex to move from mere sexual reaction to attention to the whole person. Into such love sex can be happily integrated. Thus love is the real wonder of man. It is plainly the image of God in man, the Spirit of God among men. It gives Christianity its real meaning, and the role of sex in such a religion is plainly obvious. Sex reaches its spiritual zenith in such love, as it does its highest pleasure.

CHAPTER SEVEN

Understanding Sex

To understand sex is to have a realistic awareness of the place of the genital function in the development and maturity of both the human person and the race. This includes not merely the mechanical function of the genitals but the meaning of the male-female relationship in its personal and social ramifications. The genital function alone equally involves the tsetse fly, the giant panda, the ape, and man; but human sex involves the whole meaning and purpose of man, who shares nothing essentially human with the animal world. What man is and does today, through sex, profoundly influences future generations. The heavy burden on man to make wise and right decisions of greater significance than personal pleasure or advantage requires his understanding of sex. Only deep respect for human sex can save genetics from the caprice of scientists.

The process of understanding anything has several steps. Man gets the picture through his senses (apprehends); the picture is filtered through the emotions (the impact of experience) to the mind, which understands (comprehends); accumulated understanding facilitates practical judgments through which wisdom is acquired. The end product of understanding sex is the wisdom and virtue to live well with it, to integrate it into one's loving. For the emotionally healthy person this is no problem, but for the emotionally ill, that is, the emotionally dominated or withdrawn, it is very difficult to live with sex. Battered by their clamouring emotions, they do not get the picture in the first place, or if they do, it is badly distorted. They lack almost all objectivity because they see and hear only what they like to see and hear. They are emotionally incapable of processing experience correctly; practical judgment is beyond them, and they acquire neither understanding nor wisdom. They either wallow in sex, to which they are irresistibly addicted, or withdraw in the face of it to avoid hurtful experience.

Sensing that they are made to love, they have not a clue as to how to go about it, nor any hope of achieving it; loneliness is inevitably ahead of them.

Understanding sex means much more than the knowledge and experience to achieve orgasm. Like the automobile, sex is much easier to use than to understand. Being sexually equipped carries no more right to function sexually than buying an automobile carries the right to drive. Yet most people "feel" they have a right to the pleasures and privileges of sex without the sobering responsibility to use it well. Understanding sex provides man with the knowledge required to use his over-all welfare (and that of others, which he equates with his own) rather than his "feelings" to measure the acceptability of both the pain and pleasure of sex. The mind and the will can completely control the sexual faculties, from the genitals themselves to the most urgent sexual emotions. Sex is understood when its real place in the life of man is established, and is efficaciously understood when the person actually lives that way. The man who loves accepts all the restraints on any of his sexual inclinations that are detrimental to interpersonal relationships. Understanding sex makes this possible.

The protest against those puritanical, erroneous notions of sex which retard man's growth and development as a sexual person, is legitimate. The rebellion against not only prissiness but any restraint, however, now threatens to keep man less than his genitals, since fear of sex is being replaced by sex itself as a dominant force in human living. It is no improvement to replace one form of tyranny with another. Genital sex will dominate man unless it is incorporated into loving, which is what understanding sex is all about. Happiness in sex does come from its use in a permanent, exclusive, loving relationship between man and woman. That is the one basis on which sex works really well. The problems that irresponsible and unloving sex creates in broken homes, unwanted, emotionally crippled children and the current abortion industry are but part of the high cost of misunderstood, misused sex.

The human sexual drive, unlike that in animals, is meant to accomplish the preservation of the species with love and the freedom vital to love. Everything great and wonderful about a human being should go into his sexual life. To disdain sex is to be contemptuous of man's integrity, to misunderstand the meaning of the word human. Man's happiness requires that he live happily with sex, neither suppressing nor exploiting it. He does share sex with the animals but his sex is as human as his intelligence.

The human sexual dimension enables men and women to relate to each other in a most basic way, and when sex is not understood even this simplest of interpersonal relationships is unattainable. Sex understood, however, makes it plain that the purely sexual relationship is the simplest and easiest, and therefore the least rewarding and fulfilling, of all human relationships. Those whose best performance is in the purely sexual embrace have a very limited scope indeed. Social man, however sexually active he may be, is inevitably driven into the isolation of loneliness (living suicide) when he is incapable of a loving relationship. This is very obvious in our affluent and liberal society where sex is so universally and easily available, and yet has done nothing to reduce the incredible toll of loneliness, but in fact, adds to it.

That sex education should be mandatory in these times is crystal clear. Education prepares one for life. Who doubts the importance of sex in modern life? It is plain that the functions and manifestations of sex are so confused with amorous or conjugal love that only genuine love can save most people from destruction on the jagged edges of sexual living. If sex is important, then love is much more important. There is just no way that one will understand human loving without understanding the far simpler matter of sex. Understanding sex makes it plain that the absence of genital sex is far less consequential than the absence of love. Ignorance of sex makes marriage an empty promise of paradise and celibacy a cruel, unnatural hoax, while understanding sex opens the way in marriage to deep loving rapport in the most personal relationship, and makes it possible to discover in celibacy a reasonable and fulfilling way to love. Understanding sex prevents its gross exaggeration in married love, as it prevents sex from dominating the loving relationships so vital to the celibate. It prevents sex from choking married love to death, and assures that in celibate loving nothing essentially human is missing.

The easy decision that sex education is essential does nothing to make it possible, let alone effective. Sex plays such a role in the evolution of man and his responsible behaviour- that it is far better ignored than taught badly. It seems a simple thing to have parents instruct their children in what are simplistically called "the facts of life", and few question that it is primarily their job to do so. However, even when the "facts" can be agreed upon, few parents have the understanding, the teaching know-how, or even the basic terminology of sex required for the job. Teaching sex involves much more than anatomy, physiology and biology. It involves the psychological, emotional and spiritual dimensions of man as well. The present backlash against sex education comes from the disastrous social and psychological consequences of sexual permissiveness attributed rightly and wrongly to inadequate sex education. It is a catastrophe to accept the pleasure potential of sex outside the context of society's welfare. The allusion to sex as "the facts of life" typifies the wrong approach to understanding it. There are obvious, easily verifiable facts of sex, like its anatomy and physiology, which are easily taught and learned. But there are many facets of sex and sexuality so inseparable from a sound philosophy of the purpose of man and his social life that sex education makes no sense without them. The knowledge of sexual anatomy and physiology must be directed to the complete role of sex in human life, and to the basic purpose of human life itself. Sex education must be approached also with the objectivity sought in language and science studies. Man can welcome the truth as much in his personal sexual life, if he is so disposed, as in other phases of his life. In the truth man finds his way to love as the basis of his sexual activity, when he has the goodwill to do so. Through goodwill – love – sex is fully humanized and plays its role in man's personal life and for the welfare of the race. It is the purpose of sex education to see that it does.

The power to put sex information to the best use requires more than education. And basic to human life is the realization that knowledge of facts carries no guarantee that they will be used well. Thus it is totally unrealistic to think that one who knows better will necessarily do better, since what one does depends on one's convictions and one's moral character, or virtue. Understanding sex will establish the role of sex in life but living that role requires personal principle. Many with knowledge of sex have little ability, desire or intention to use it for anything but their own enjoyment, which takes it completely out of the context of real life. But sex *has* to be lived well; sex really matters in public as well as private life, to a much greater degree than almost any academic subject. Thus sex education by hedonists, who through arrogance or ignorance dismiss the moral aspects of sex, has to be unacceptable. Their contempt for restraints other than those acceptable to themselves disqualifies them as sex educators. Those who too glibly pass on their own limited and badly thought-out ideas, their peculiar hang-ups and behaviour patterns, violate their trust as teachers. Sex made a matter of pure academics is taken out of life's context and the way is opened to exploitative pleasure addiction. Plainly, sex education requires teachers of extraordinary insight, intelligence, understanding and moral goodness. It is obviously a formidable undertaking.

Most parents trust only those sex educators having a deep understanding of the whole subject in all its ramifications, for whom sex is a matter of personal convictions as well as social concern. This involves an appreciation of moral values originating in the history of sex and contributing to the wisdom to avoid the devastating misuse of sex. The prophets of the new sexual freedom, ignoring essential moral values, actually preach a new kind of slavery. While invoking cultural and religious superstition to justify throwing off every restrictive obligation, they provide no answers to the problems of pleasure addiction, sexual licence, and the incredible devastation of unloving. The deadly results of incomplete sex instruction are most obvious only when the headlong course to personal destruction is all but irreversible.

Another problem in sex education is the narrow, proud person who tolerates mistakes in general learning but is strangely intolerant of even honest mistakes in learning sex. Sex education carries no special dispensation from error, even for those who wish it did. Sexual mistakes, far from being catastrophic or irremediable, often supply in humility what is lost in chastity; they do carry with them the learning value which St. Augustine so thoroughly appreciated, often occasioning a healthy compensatory honesty. While no formal sex education can take the place of good example, parents, teachers, counselors and friends contribute immensely to emotional maturity and personal growth by helping others to recognize, accept and learn by their mistakes. Sex education can never be the exclusive responsibility of any one institution or person.

Proper sex education should prepare the way for the inevitable sexual experience of the developing child. It can be categorically stated that the reaction of the child to sexual experience is the same as his reaction to any other normal experience, except where, through ignorance or prejudice, he has been conditioned to apprehension or fear of sex, or led prematurely by seduction into sexual indulgence. The child can be disposed to sexual pleasure addiction by his acquired emotional reactions to pain and pleasure. Indulgence in pleasure rewards by misguided parents is just as prejudicial to learning through sexual experience as is punishing a frightened child surprised in some sexual discovery. The child not already addicted to pleasure seldom finds the pleasure of sex irresistible.

Ideally the child should learn as quickly and well as possible to accept fully the fact of sex, to understand its urgency and compulsion at the feeling level, without being deluded that it is beyond control, or that control is unnecessary. Psychiatrists, psychologists and counselors who dismiss masturbation as unimportant, as having little or no symptomatic significance, deprive the child of the understanding needed for the sexual control indispensable to emotionally healthy living. Healthy acceptance of sexual experience is vital in acquiring the power to direct all lesser functions to the good of the whole person and of society. While the child discovered at masturbation should not be threatened, neither should he be awarded a medal. He should be intelligently guided to interests outside himself which absorb the attention otherwise wasted on self-pity and self-indulgence. Children who are starved for affection, who have experienced rejection, real or imagined, are severely handicapped in the initial discovery of genital pleasure. They are often, or even generally, inclined to turn in to themselves, in masturbation, as a compensatory pleasure mechanism, with varying but always undesirable results.

Masturbation is begun for any number of reasons, from a quite innocent, accidental discovery of easily available and ever accessible pleasure, to the prankish, seductive explorations encouraged by peers or older companions. Subsequent studies seem to support Kinsey's figures for masturbation – that is, that 90% of boys and 50% of girls masturbate any number of times from once to habitually. Those who masturbate only once, or rarely, can in no way be considered *bona fide* masturbators. They certainly do not bear the emotional scars of sexual pleasure addiction. They have no delusions about the urgency or inevitability of sexual misuse. Kinsey's figures do indicate, however, the extent of the undiscriminating search of children for pleasure rewards (much wants more), which they must learn to accept when beneficial, and to deny themselves when prejudicial. It is utterly ridiculous to accept masturbation, however statistically normal, as a healthy, harmless outlet for emotional tensions. Like a temper tantrum, masturbation is one way of releasing emotional pressure but it does not replace emotional control. Only the mistake of equating emotional control with emotional repression makes masturbation seem preferable to worse things. At best, it is always only the lesser of evils. It is usually an early symptom of predisposition to addiction. The emotional health of the child requires willingness to accept his failures; and masturbation, like a temper tantrum, is a failure. No failure is commendable, however understandable and acceptable as a fact. Despite statistics, masturbation, like the measles, is not made good because of the number experiencing it. Statistical games contribute nothing to the development of children into emotionally healthy adults.

A crucial stage in understanding sex is reached in the sexual experience of puberty, the physiological plea of sex for recognition and acceptance. As sexual maturity begins in the emotionally unrepressed person, pleasurable sexual feelings increase their pressure in the livelier flow and ebb of blood through the muscles and nerves of the sexual sensory centres. This experiential awareness of the sex pleasure factor is essential to maturity. At this time sexual needs are felt with a highly exciting and compelling novelty. Curiosity, the stimulus to understanding, is unusually high. The growing boy experiences full erections both in his sleep and while awake, resulting from internal and external physical and psychological stimuli. Those who deplore or dread this "thrust from innocence to experience" would delay maturity and deprive the boy of the very experience vital to understanding and coping with sex. To cope with sex means to develop the necessary control to live successfully with it.

Unprovoked nocturnal seminal emissions, as pleasurable as, and usually involving, orgasm, take place with some regularity in the boy, with a force which alerts him to his manhood and its responsibilities. Inherent in the experience of the erection is the dawning comprehension of the sexual purpose for his penis, and a strong new awareness of the desire to so use it. He may or may not masturbate or have intercourse, but even where moral principles and self-discipline are sufficient for continence, it is important that through the experience of the erection and emission, the place of sex in his life is gradually understood and fully accepted. He gradually comprehends sex as the combined operation of two free, responsible people bringing to the act not only their functional equipment but enough mutual love and respect to establish a lasting relationship. This relationship provides the secure atmosphere into which children ought to be born.

The same basic process takes place in the girl, though not necessarily with the same conscious awareness. The Western cultural penalty on the "good" woman for discussing sex openly only partially explains her lag in conscious awareness, knowledge and acceptance of sex. She should be helped to understand what her body is trying to make plain, that she wants the love of a man, a home, and his child. She too becomes acutely aware of the flow and ebb of sexual sensation in her body and should know the precise meaning of these sensations. The increased flow of blood to her clitoris and other genital organs makes her aware of sexual pleasure and her basic need for sexual fulfilment. She also experiences the pressing sexual needs normal to her menstrual cycle. She senses a vaginal emptiness, and an expectant, eager readiness for intercourse, a physical, psychological and personal anxiety to be filled. As with her brothers, it is most important for her, too, to use these experiences to gradually understand and accept the place of sex in her life, and its relationship to loving. Each sex should be made aware of the parallel experience of the opposite sex, which seems so different but which in reality is so much the same. These sexual experiences are essentially the bases of understanding sex.

The normal man is attracted to women, and considers, however fleetingly, having intercourse with every woman to whom he is attracted. He falls easily in love with one, and probably several, women, both before and after his commitment to marriage. If he is mature, thoughtful and disciplined he will be deeply in love with the one he marries. He should, however, freely consider having intercourse with other women, that is to say, insist that his mind follow, constructively and responsibly, the train of thought suggested by his feelings. It is when he looks at the sex act in the context of the relationship, rather than in isolated fantasy, that the occasion for the virtue of fidelity is presented, that he is challenged to place the emphasis on the person rather than the body. By nature man wants the intercourse for which he is born and equipped; his normal inclination is to have intercourse often and with many women. It is when he thinks the matter through (which requires little time, and should not be confused with daydreaming, or wallowing in visions of a thousand and one nights of sexual delights) and imagines that he has had intercourse with the one attracting him, that he then asks himself how such an act can be reconciled with true love, his present obligations, and the real good of the persons involved. Honest answers easily disabuse him of delusions, expose philandering for what it is and make plain the impossible complications it introduces into real life. Only the dreamer or escapist can see advantages in contradictions to true love, in taking sex out of the context of reality, the loving relationship. It is easy to have intercourse, but to be meaningful it must be had with one to whom one relates deeply and personally. Promiscuity makes a shambles of one's personal relations and one's happiness. Sexual experience makes this plain; it also makes plain how meaningful intercourse is in the living security of the lasting commitment.

Fundamental to understanding sex is the conviction that man is greater than sex – its master, not its slave. Those exploiting others for personal pleasure twist themselves beyond recognition as human.

Morally, they should be pariahs; but our society is a sick one which ostracizes only the visibly ugly, in which it is much less acceptable to smell bad than to be bad. Any reasonable man accepts restraints on his temper; restraints on his sexual life are even more reasonable. The social aspect of sexual life is inescapable and therefore never anyone's private business. Society is the beneficiary of sexual life; it is the milieu of sexual existence. Sex has no meaning when restricted to the individual, therefore it can never be a matter of personal whim. Sex is always disordered unless the whole man grows through it. It must likewise increase the stature of his partner and of society. Other individuals, and society, suffer from the sex-dominated man or woman. The part that exploitative sex plays in crime and the rackets is obvious. The taxable income from crime would provide half the required operating expense of modern government. But the real tax paid on commercial sex, perversion, and addictive pleasure is the reduced stature of man himself.

Neither is sex merely for breeding. A great disservice is rendered sex when the physical production of children is made a virtue in itself. A subfunction of man's dominant powers to think and to love, sex is degraded when used in a thoughtless or unloving way. It is not a matter merely of instinct, physiological or biological drive, or emotional compulsion – not an end in itself, justified by the thrills it provides. It is a highly human act which, when done lovingly, may produce loved and loving children. The sexual controls built into man are enough to assure it being so used by anyone wanting to so use it. To do so man merely needs the motivation, the convictions of a loving person.

The built-in sexual controls are well illustrated by the physiology of blushing. (It has been wisely stated that man is the only creature who blushes, and the only one with reason to.) Blushing indicates emotional insecurity, undue shame or embarrassment. One simply cannot blush if he is relaxed; one need not blush if he is controlled. A blush is the retention of blood in the head as the heart pumps faster and the return flow to the heart is restricted by tension. Pressure forces the dammed-up blood to the facial tissues. On relaxation the dam opens, normal circulation returns and the blushing ceases. A similar tension is equally required for the erection of the penis or the clitoris. When sex is understood there is very early awareness of sexual excitement; the mind moves into action and the will takes control, if desired, well before full sexual arousal occurs. When one is motivated by a greater good (or desire) the simple command to relax causes the sexual arousal to quickly subside. The same physical effect can be experienced when the attention is diverted to something more pressing or urgent, including what is demanded by the best interests of the stimulated or stimulator. Sexual arousal is interrupted by any more dominant stimulus, such as the external threat of force or some urgent contingency. Anyone who has as much motivation to reduce sexual arousal as he has to control blushing, stuttering or any other emotional manifestation based on the tension of excitement, has adequate controls at his disposal to love well without getting bogged down in sex.

Those who deny this control are either incredibly self-indulgent, or are unaware of man's ability to master any voluntary situation in which he finds himself, or simply have no desire to use self-control. The person who can accept pleasure without being carried away by it readily accepts the built-in mechanisms of sexual control. For him, it is self-evident that sexual fulfilment consists not in using sex as one wishes, pleases or feels, but in achieving a happy life. Pleasure itself is purely experiential not a moral matter; its use is a matter of wisdom and judgment. The best management of pleasure and pain is the only reason for everyman's innate power of self-control. Every function of man is essentially controllable by him. Certainly when a stronger emotion so easily inhibits a weaker one, the will obviously can control them all. Thus love and hate provide the strongest motivations of man and both can certainly dominate the genital function even in the most erotic situations.

It is easy to find numerous other examples of sexual inhibition, or control. Sickness or hormone imbalance can cause temporary impotence. The inhibiting factors in psychological impotence, or frigidity, are plainly obvious. Any dominating emotion – fear, anger, resentment, or even indifference – inhibits the sexual emotions, for the simple reason that the inhibiting power is there. Similar specific control mechanisms in the body are the basis for the fantastic control exotic dancers exercise over individual muscles. Some very recent experiments on the autonomic nervous systems of rats have demonstrated their ability to control, for food reward, not only their own heart rate and blood pressure but even the vasodilation of the blood vessels of their right or left ears! Man certainly has these controls at his disposal too; he needs only the motivation and discipline to use them. He will hopefully be inspired to do so when he understands sex sufficiently to accept that it is tied primarily into his personal life of happiness, and then into his emotional life of pleasure.

The compelling force of sex is generally accepted as all but irresistible because it generally is not resisted. Either sufficient motive, or the required self-discipline, or the understanding of the control mechanisms is lacking. The actual compulsion to sex is attributed to sex itself instead of to the contagious nature of sexual excitement. But laughter and tears are as contagious and compelling as sexual excitement, to say nothing of nausea. Few can resist nausea in the presence of a violently vomiting person, yet it is quite controllable. The stimulus can be killed by changing one's focus from it. Intense interest in the sick person cuts right across the stimulus of nausea, as does joy in being of help, or the satisfaction of helping in the rejection of the sickening substance. Doctors, nurses and other attendants of the sick become so conditioned to resist nausea that they are all but immune to its stimulus. A disciplined, strong-willed person can remain relaxed and calm, and so place himself beyond the stimulus of sexual excitement. Naturally, the greatest incentive to do that is the true and deep love of a person whose real good excludes the sexual function temporarily or even permanently. However, to control sexual excitement one must be a strong person, and if not a virtuous, at least a very proud person. But the potential control is there, given the motive, the goodwill, and the understanding of the control processes related to the sexual function.

The incredibly sensitive nerves of the sexual organs do respond beautifully to physical and psychological stimuli, but neither necessarily nor automatically. All nerve control centres including the sexual ones are governed by the cerebral cortex, the computer programmed by the mind. Yet most people doubt the possibility of handling sexual excitement maturely and responsibly because they believe they must be carried irresistibly to genital climax regardless of its wisdom, emptiness, wrongness, or even criminality. Although sexual domination is prejudicial and personally destructive, and ultimately leads to unhappiness, few accept that sexual control is possible, let alone desirable or necessary.

If sexual arousal on stimulation were automatic, how could the psychologically impotent man or frigid woman be explained? How explain the man who performs well privately but simply cannot do so publicly? The control of the male gynaecologist examining patients? The unacceptability of sexual overtures is generally enough to inhibit sex arousal. The most sensual person can be temporarily impotent because greater emotional pressure focuses his attention elsewhere. Few people could respond sexually in a busy shopping plaza, however excited they might become about the same person in other circumstances. The nerve sensations from the sexual organs can be ignored whenever there is sufficient reason for doing so, as any husband who has vainly tried to stimulate an indifferent wife has learned. The loving person has the best motives in the world for exercising his sexual inhibiting powers; the indulgent, promiscuous, selfish person has little or none. This tremendous power of emotional control is rediscovered and developed by every alcoholic, chain smoker, compulsive eater or habitual masturbator who faces the truth and does what he knows is best, regardless of his feelings.

Sexual inhibition for inhibition's sake is ridiculous, but who would accuse a loving mother of being ridiculous when she terminates sexual intercourse to go quickly to an injured child? Who would criticize the loving spouse from refraining from intercourse when his mate is ill or injured? In similar vein, the celibate is not abusing his sexual inhibiting power when he invokes it, to an extent which precludes marriage and a family of his own, to serve others lovingly for life.

However compelling or pleasurable sexual intercourse may be, man has the potential intelligence, goodwill and physical controls to choose to function sexually or not, according to whether it is in his own best interests, those of others, or those of society itself. Many people, in the face of an attractive invitation to sexual intercourse, decline because of fidelity to their partners, the unwisdom of involvement, fear of subsequent betrayal or of getting caught. The fact that chastity seems unusual in our society does not discount the power to be chaste, but merely indicates the lack of sufficient understanding, motivation, discipline and love.

The person who recognizes, accepts and learns to live with his sexual emotions will understand sex fairly well. The male must feel like a male, and the female like a female. Such feelings make living as a fully human being the challenge that it is. To reject this challenge and accept one's sexual function on a purely pleasure level is to function subhumanly. Understanding sex demands the mature acceptance of the inherent sexual attraction always present in the development of intersexual relationships. This acceptance then requires the self-discipline to direct the sexual life lovingly. All sexual stimuli can be neutralized, or dominated, by stronger stimuli to contrary emotions. The ferocious knock of the jealous husband on the door of the hideaway lovenest certainly creates very sexually inhibiting emotions. However, to promote other strong emotions, such as fear, to control sexual desires is disastrous, since such action assures immaturity and instability. Misuse of the emotions can never replace the real virtue and character through which loving people use sexually inhibiting mechanisms properly for the right reasons. The puritanical atmosphere of the strict home, and the moral family environment of the small town, because they more often developed fear than virtue, were poor preparations for urban living with its swinging society and permissive anonymity.

Sex can never be understood by those attributing moral qualities to the sexual emotions. Many "good" people consider sexual feelings occasions of sin, or temptations. They are seen as a threat to virtue rather than as awakening one to the beginnings of a relationship. These people have been generally brainwashed into believing that sex is bigger than man, and they either accept the inevitability of being carried away by the most normal sexual feelings, or they freeze in the face of them and allow themselves to be driven from a loving situation by their feelings. People of high moral awareness often tend to morbid fear of the genuine tenderness which elicits sexual feelings akin to those experienced in erotic situations. The minor genital discharge experienced through loving tenderness puts them into severe anxiety, even panic. Yet it is as normal as the tear shed in joy or sorrow; it need have no erotic significance whatever. When such a mechanical reaction is dismissed for what it is, having no more significance than a blush, the sex feelings remain minimal, and anxiety vanishes. Panic does nothing to help one distinguish fear from guilt or anxiety, but easily magnifies feelings into motives, blows mechanical responses into deliberate acts, converts pleasure into sin, thus making understanding of sex impossible. Anxiety creates tension which exaggerates any emotional response, including the sexual, and makes the physical effects more difficult to cope with and the psychological aftermath often devastating. Such reactions, blown out of all proportion by misunderstood, mismanaged emotions, often create the fear, in perfectly good people, that they are, potentially at least, satyrs or nymphomaniacs.

Normal sexual emotions are the occasion of the practice of chastity. The person with suppressed sexual emotions thus does not acquire the virtue of chastity against the time when it is needed. On the other hand, when anxiety, guilt, fear and shame accompany the most normal sexual feelings, the power of sex has to seem overwhelming, and the practice of chastity impossible. Sexual feelings are normally present in all interpersonal relationships and are the very stuff of chastity. The sexual emotions quickly reveal to the mature, virtuous person the nature of the situation he is in, and he refuses to be frightened from the challenge to love by the small degree of sexual agitation he feels. All sexual situations present the risk of tragic mistakes, but no greater mistake can be made than letting the sexual emotions drive one from the loving situation which requires the virtue of chastity to assure its development.

The emotions provide the pieces of the jigsaw puzzle of life, and with the help of the imagination the mind programs them through the computer of the brain. It takes considerable imagination to understand the place of the emotions in life, to so program pain and pleasure into real life that the former is not rejected when beneficial and the latter not indulged in when harmful. There is a general tendency to short-circuit the imagination's vital role in understanding, a role which is especially important in understanding sex. When through ignorance of its function it is wasted, the imagination is easily made the scapegoat for all kinds of abuses.

A function of the mind, the imagination is not the mind, nor the emotions, nor fantasy, which is its work. It is the faculty of ingenuity, inventiveness. Vision gestates in the womb of the imagination to deliver progress. It produced the tools with which man built, and arranged the sounds with which he communicated and the numbers with which he counted, measured and weighed. Every useful invention of man is evidence of the imagination well used. It is the faculty of projection and planning. To understand sex, the mind must get the picture. The imagination is the picture tube pulling the intellectual and sensitive memories together, relating the experiences required for ingenious thinking. Genital sex requires little if any imagination. It functions automatically, unless inhibited, in response to physical or psychological stimuli. Imagination negotiates genital sex to love. It provides the blueprints for authentic loving situations in which man learns to give despite every inclination to get. The imagination previews the emotional stimuli experienced in related fields and makes it possible to anticipate and manage any normal venture into loving.

Before the imagination can program sex into the loving process, it must liberate one from the ridiculous domination of sex which makes man, momentarily at least, less than his genitals. The imagination does have the power to seduce, to present graphically orgies of unlimited delight, but only when it is abused rather than used. It is the unimaginative who can be enticed by the strip tease. A little imagination reveals what the tease addict hopes to see, and explodes the false promise. The imagination lays out quite clearly all that sex has to offer and finds it wanting, for sex is not all people want. Those who understand sex are not deceived by its limited dividends. The imagination can take one through the mirage of sexual pleasure to the very real happiness of love. The most imaginative use of sex is not by the people who indulge sexually but by those who use sex commercially to exploit the unimaginative. Imaginative people quickly recognize the phony and are seldom deluded by a one dimensional situation. Wise people do not fall for something as easily explored and quickly exhausted as sex, but placing sex into the context of real life they move ahead imaginatively to achieve loving relationships, visualizing the true needs of others and the means of fulfilling them. The imagination provides the plans through which love is fruitful and rewarding.

The imagination, like sex, is meant to be the servant, rather than the master, of the man. However, it must be made to serve rather than let run riot, as it does in the lives of the undisciplined. One bogged down in sexual fantasies is sick. Imagination gone wild can so isolate sex from real life that it appears great in itself. Sexual pleasure can seem like an adequate reward for the intolerable situations it leads to, or the heartbreaks inseparable from it outside the context of love. The fear of using the imagination badly, born of sad experience, unfortunately leads many to believe that it cannot be used well.

The mind uses the imagination to produce the master plan for understanding sex, and from that plan lays out the man-hours of constructive work required for handling sex properly, integrating it into love and life. Applied to personal relationships, a well used imagination clearly portrays, in time for correction, the disaster of sexual compulsion, the chaos of unresisted sexual desire. It presents with compelling clarity the comparison of the fleeting pleasure of orgasm with the enduring happiness and security of love. It makes it clear that the genitals, like the imagination itself, cannot fulfil their function when used like a toy, for one's own amusement. Only those people who misuse the imagination to build their own dream worlds of escape could delude themselves that sex can be equated either with personal relationships or with happiness. The divorce courts are clogged with marriages, based on sexual attraction, which a little imagination would have exposed as hopeless from the beginning. The number of departed celibates could have been cut in half if those leaving for the joys of marriage would have imagined how little sex had to offer people whose trouble was the inability to love. Certainly had imagination been used to anticipate the problems, and inspire the virtue so basic to celibate life, celibate commitment could never have eroded as it has today.

The runaway imagination, like the loan shark, insists that you can play now and pay later; the directed imagination tells you just how much you will pay later. The imagination, which created the myth of sex appeal for commercial purposes, can also explode it, debunk promises which cannot be kept, expose relationships which are dead ends. It also reveals the cultural hang-ups and ignorance which portray women as being more interested in love and less interested in sex, deeper, more faithful, virtuous and religious than men. The properly operating imagination shows men and women as made for each other, much more alike as human beings than different. They are necessarily alike because they are complementary. The imagination sees it as the way of woman to open up personally, much more than sexually, to the personal penetration of the man she loves. And this is counterparted by the equal eagerness of the man to open up to the personal penetration of the woman's love which envelops him. The knowledgeable woman (and no one is knowledgeable without an efficacious imagination) is very aware that no sexual opening is nearly as important as her personal opening in love. Her qualities as a person, friend and companion are far more valued by her than those of her body. She does not depend on externals, deceit, beauty aids or psychological cover-ups which betray her insecurity. It is plain to her that an attractive person's body is *always* attractive, for beauty is a personal rather than a physical thing.

The woman understanding sex appreciates the vulnerability of her body to the thrust of a man. She knows that her real protection is his love for her, his trust in her. But she also appreciates the man's vulnerability to her psychological thrust. He too knows that the only protection he has from hurt is the love of the woman for him. Men and women are equally vulnerable and interdependent; both are capable of deep hurt from misplaced trust. The directed imagination presents this cold reality to both lover and loved, warning them against the disaster of premature sexual involvement.

Sex appeal in no way assures enduring relationships, and in fact deflects the genuine interest of the best and most discerning people. Experience sadly reveals how seldom a real person lives behind the facade of physical beauty. Physically attractive people, often unable to inspire or maintain personal relationships, need promiscuity to keep sex from becoming a complete bore. Boredom is impossible in love and friendship because of the continuing discovery of new dimensions of personality. The imaginative find the exploration of another person far more exciting, challenging and rewarding than the exploration of a body. A body can share sex but it takes a person to share love.

Understanding sex makes it plain how love is short-circuited by overeagerness to copulate. The apostles of sex are emotional children, forever eating the icing off the cake. Those who do not understand sex mine it for every last sliver of pleasure while love goes down the drain. However interesting, sex is a brief experience; love is a lasting experience with an interesting person. The directed imagination fastens the precise limits of sexual pleasure and relates sex correctly to the loving life.

The study of sex, undertaken by thoughtful, able people of integrity, will clear the way to the study of the power to love. More than anything else, unreasonable delay led those unwilling to be dominated by sex to choose, unhappily, not to love at all. The mature man, through love, enters a sexual union with a woman whom he chooses because of her lovable qualities. Their relationship neither begins nor ends with the sexual one but endures and matures in a personal relationship with common interests, eagerness to share in a lasting personal commitment. To understand and use sex properly man must see that he can, and decide that he will, love. Unfortunately, man's intelligence is much better developed than his goodwill. To operate for something more than his immediate personal pleasure demands an accepted set of standards, and virtue – the power to do what ought to be done. Without these love will remain the secret of a very few.

To understand sex means to function better not only sexually but personally. Man functions best when genuinely loving, which he cannot be without understanding sex. Ignorance of sex is not merely a tremendous obstacle to loving, but even to relating to other people, which is the beginning of love. When that obstacle has been removed the way to love is open. When science accepts the real relationship of man's genitals to his power to love, behavioural scientists will refuse to discuss human sex apart from love.

CHAPTER EIGHT

The Power to Love

Nowhere is the image of God in man so evident as in the deep, loving interpersonal relationship in which one human being looks at another and loves him. Man is never happier or more fulfilled, more virtuous and less vicious than when he loves. He is never more of a man, or a better person, than when he is keenly aware of, and most willing to fulfil, the true needs of his fellow man. This is love. God is truly manifest in the man who loves endlessly, simply because he can see God in all, any man, every man. Such love soon uncovers the image of God in one's unlovable neighbour and then works its miracle of changing unloving man to loving man.

Loving is the source of all man's happiness, as distinct from his pleasure. Only loving man is a genuine man of peace. He alone has security enough to see and confront his prejudices. Love is the broad base of all interested personal relationships. It is man's happiness to look out and away from himself, to see all that is beautiful and good, and to feel the privilege of living in the midst of it all, contributing to it, giving out from his depths, sharing, loving. Through the power of love man empties himself of the sadness of failure and fills himself with the joy that is out there, sensing that it is all big and wonderful and made for him, wanting desperately to be a real part of it all.

The power to love underlies man's prayer life, his ability to relate to God, the maker of all things, with a deep sense of gratitude for being. Who cannot thank God for that cannot love, because he cannot get his attention off himself, either to God or to man. He is too sick to see the other person.

To doubt the value or count the cost of loving is to deny God. The belief that Christ is God in flesh, the expressed Love of God, God's Word made flesh, is supported by His teaching. His message was quite worthy of God, that man should love, would find his fulfilment in loving. Jesus said: "You must love the Lord your God with all your heart, with all your soul, and with all your mind. This is the greatest and the first commandment. The second resembles it: you must love your neighbour as yourself. On these two commandments hang the whole Law and the Prophets also." (Matthew 22:37-40).

Great men have shown by devoting their whole lives, even dying for their neighbour, that such love is certainly possible, fulfilling and rewarding. The problem of loving is always the cost. Wealth, intelligence, energy and time build a better material world, but self is the cost of a loving world, giving not one's substance but oneself. Man must be willing to lose himself to find himself, was the way Christ put it. Money cannot eliminate poverty, hunger or discrimination; dedicated, loving people can. People who want to be somebody without spending themselves are shocked when St. Paul tells them plainly that unloving people are nothing, nobodies. Life without loving is nothing.

Christ was very clear about how man should pass through the emotional bogs of self-indulgence which keep him subhuman, unloving. He said: "You have learned how it was said: You must love your neighbour and hate your enemy. But I say this to you: love your enemies and pray for those who persecute you; in this way will you be sons of your Father in heaven . . . For if you love those who love you what right have you to claim any credit? Even the tax-collectors do as much do they not?" (Matthew 5:43-47) Was Christ asking the impossible? As a matter of fact, the person who will not love his enemies will never love his friends. Both loves require the same quality, virtue – that is, the power to do what ought to be done regardless of one's feelings.

Love, as used in this book, is the power to see and the willingness to fulfil the true needs of another. This definition removes the apparent contradiction of loving one's enemies. Love is the power to do what is good for the other person, friend or enemy. After all one feels as strongly inclined to exploit one's friends as to destroy one's enemies. Both feelings give one equal pleasure, the same kind of delight. Love, on the contrary, consists in doing right by all. The young man feels the desire to copulate with the young lady he claims to love, as strongly as he feels the desire to crush his enemies. The love that makes it plain to him that he cannot take advantage of one he loves makes it equally plain that he cannot take advantage of an enemy.

Love demands the objectivity to equate the needs of anyone, acquaintance or stranger, friend or foe, with one's own. It demands the discipline to treat even strangers and enemies as human beings, with the dignity and respect due them as fellow men, brothers and sisters. It demands the wisdom to differentiate between real needs and wishes or emotional desires. Love distinguishes between fulfilment and enjoyment by giving rightness and goodness priority over pleasure and pain. Actually the key word in loving is *goodwill*. The loving man has always the ability to will the good of the other person; he is prepared to pay the real cost of peace, however great.

Peace was promised by the angels at the birth of Christ to men of *goodwill*, that is, to loving men. Peace on any other terms is a contradiction, a mere truce in the fighting for the convenience of both parties. Imposed peace is conquest. There can be peace in the world only when treaties are negotiated by people on each side intent on achieving the best interests of the other side, which they rightly and wisely identify with their own. The armed standoff, as the whole world knows only too well, is very expensive and always temporary. Many world leaders were convinced that the brutality and carnage of war would make men of peace, convert them to love. The man in history's streets, too, wanted to believe that victory would bring lasting peace. But real peace never comes until each man exercises his own will to be good, to love rather than to hate. Love disarms enemies at so much less cost than war! It is all but impossible to discover why man puts so much more effort into hate and death than into love and life. The evidence is overwhelming that man lacks not the intelligence but the goodwill, the love for real peace.

What is this power to love? It is the power by which a man sees the good of each other person as equal to his own, makes the good of each other person his purpose, his goal. Any particular or special love comes only from a broad base of general loving. Love, like man himself, begins small, with a gentle, outgoing interest in all the others one comes in contact with, and then spreads from a broad base of general loving until its intensity and power reach another individual in such understanding that they become one in a way far surpassing a mere physical relationship. Their minds and wills, their spirits, are one; their work, ambitions and interests are one, though each retains his individuality, his wholeness. Their union excludes no one, makes room for all who need them, who can appreciate and share the virtually inexhaustible riches they find in love.

Love can neither be legislated nor compelled, but is a person-to-person voluntary relationship. It is not necessarily a mutual relationship, though through complete misunderstanding of love, most people refuse to believe love is possible when unreturned. Love is a free man's offering of himself in service to another, regardless of whether that service is accepted or even acknowledged. Love is the power to make an outright gift, not a trade. Love given for love returned is a contradiction. Love is the ability to see and the willingness to fulfil the true needs of another *without return.* Thus the loving person is quite capable of loving the unloving as well as the loving. Love given generally does evoke love in return from those secure enough to love, but the degree of the love returned depends on the maturity of the loved one and his glad recognition of the goodness of the lover. The love relationship is neither a fifty-fifty proposition nor a two-way street. It is two one-way streets, two 100% unilateral gifts, each lover functioning independently with maximum concern for the other and minimum concern for self.

Love is the power by which man handles all situations successfully and directs all relationships for the good and happiness of other people, while respecting their freedom and integrity. It is the power by which a person is open and responsive to truth, beauty and goodness. Through it parents serve their children without spoiling them; children respond to their parents without surrendering their identity; man serves God, society, nation, neighbours and family with freedom in the process of growth. Love is the greatest quality of a real person, and the only one which can inspire and hold the love and respect of another. Love is the one thing in which disappointment is impossible. It is the unshakeable personal security which lets one invest in another without fear or loss, enables one to absorb rejection with understanding. Even in those capable of little favourable response, true love by its very generosity gradually awakens and inspires such a sense of their own power to love that they begin to look at other people in a way they have never experienced. They are like the blind given sight, looking on a new world of lovable people to be loved. The miracle of loving uncovers and enlivens the spark of self-esteem and worth in every man. Regardless of its romantic poetry and music, love is not an accident. It is the finest deliberate act of a fully responsible human being, and so, the highest tribute one person can pay to another. The power to love, put simply, is the ability to be governed in all that is thought, said or done by the best interests of others, rather than by conventions, politics, respect of person, self-interest or trade. Love is above the law, it requires the minimum because it assures the maximum. Love is not lawless but flawless.

Love is expansive and diffusive rather than exclusive and possessive.

It is that quality in a person which forces its way out, seeks others, is interested in others, therefore takes the emphasis off oneself and relieves one of the miseries which come from bare existence in the prison of self-pity, anxiety and loneliness. It shares itself without being reduced, threatened or lost. It can never be restricted to or possessed by one person for it is genuinely interested in, and outgoing to, all. It is neither obstrusive nor invasive; it respects the rights and privileges of all, including their privacy. Everyone who loves has a tremendous sense of really living, of eager aliveness, of having found the purpose in life, of seeing the meaning in things. This sense is what makes it possible to absorb rejection and punishment without bitterness, to suffer while still feeling privileged. Actually, love is the quality underlying all conviction about immortality, for there is something about true love which makes it invulnerable, impervious even to death, enduring beyond any reasoned limit. Thus, loving people never run out of hope.

Man is meant to copulate because he is born with the equipment to do so. What is not so plainly obvious is that man is equally born with the equipment to think and to love, and that it is as natural for him to think and to love as it is for him to copulate. Omitting for a moment the darkness of the mind and weakness of the will consequential to original sin, a child comes into the world without prejudice or scars, anxious only to get free of the womb and into the world, expecting to be well loved and cared for. If it is warmly and tenderly received it will move naturally into a loving way of life. A child is born of its first teacher, its mother, and into its first classroom, its home. Church, school and society are secondary influences however profound they may be. If the children of well-mannered, educated people are off to a first-rate academic start, the valued children of loving parents are on their way to being the best emotionally adjusted in the world.

Emotional security derives from the sense of personal worth with which a child comes into the world and which loving parents carefully nurture to maturity. Born with a basic goodness, a value, the child becomes aware of it as a sense of its own worth. It is the first thing, apart from life itself, to flourish or wither according to the environment in which it finds itself. The sense of worth will persist and thrive to the degree that the child is loved for it. It is as if a child were born into an inheritance of spiritual wealth. If real love is lavished on the child that inheritance increases in leaps and bounds. If that child senses itself to be unwanted and unloved its inheritance is so dissipated and dispersed that virtually no sense of worth remains. Deeply loving parents bring out this sense of worth in a child so strongly that it can seldom ever be lost. But unless it is brought out it is doubtful that that child will ever be a whole person or ever succeed in loving anyone well.

Social scientists have concluded that emotional health is largely determined in the first year of life. It has been generally observed that babies thrive emotionally who have been gladly breast-fed, because loving attention is their earliest experience, which registers primarily, of course, on their feelings. Emphasis should be on the "gladly" rather than "breast-fed" because grudging breast feeding by selfish, uninterested mothers is less desirable than interested bottle feeding by nurses. The point is that when the breasts are gladly used for the function for which they are designed the infant gets the message clearly that it is loved and wanted, it receives loving interest which it is being very much emotionally conditioned to return just as gladly.

The basic ability to love is seen in the early capacity to be interested in others. That interest is the broad base of loving without which the potential to love would not develop. Every encouragement should be given children to go out to others, to cooperate with them and contribute to their best interests. This is the actual disposition of the child warmly received into a loving home. This child will not be thrown off by fear of a rejection it has not experienced in infancy.

Because God is Love, there are hardly more hypocritical words than "I love you" used to prove devotion to another while exploiting that person for one's own satisfaction. "I love you" are words almost universally used to express physical, sexual attraction to someone, the desire to possess that person sexually as soon as possible. As mouthed by so many, they signify so much greater desire to take than to give that even children quickly recognize the hypocrisy in them. They are used hypocritically by parents to impose their wills on their children, to compel affection, to beg tolerance, or to project their own ambitions on their children. They are used in turn by the children to bribe or seduce their parents into gifts, or to insinuate their own wills. They are used, with incredible shallowness, in the entertainment and commercial worlds for the benefit of those who pay the most. They are used by citizens in general to protest their love of country, always used loudest when there is least demand on them personally and the greatest benefit from merely being citizens. What "I love you" really ought to mean is, "You are of the highest importance to me. Your welfare has high priority in my life. I respect you as I respect myself. I will share not only my possessions with you, but my life." Obviously, whoever can tell another he loves, and be speaking the truth, is as superb as he is rare.

Despite the use of love in reference to God, neighbours, parents, children, brothers and sisters, and even native country, many people today still automatically assume that sex and love are one. One result of this is that, since sex is easy, love is likewise assumed to be easy. Love also seems deceptively easy because it is so readily confused with falling or being "in love", an emotional state of euphoria, delight. The emotions of love and the delights of sexual pleasure, purely personal sensations, are to most people the only infallible signs of deep personal love. Those who have fallen in love two or three times know perfectly well that the delightful expectations of a deep personal relationship to follow are generally empty and unwarranted ones. Highly charged, emotional beginnings seldom stand the test of time and generally lead nowhere. Sex requires only the most superficial of relationships, with very quickly reached physical limits. Love is a relationship of unlimited depth, innumerable ramifications revealing the persons involved to each other indefinitely in new ways and depths.

'One who settles for genital pleasure as an end in itself writes off the happiness of love.' However great the undoubted pleasure of sex, the purely mechanical functions of the genital organs can never be a high human achievement. Sex feelings do give the impetus to relate to another person but they are merely occasions, never causes, of a loving relationship. Personal reform stimulated by sex is never improvement but mere accommodation, self-interested adaptation. Sex is dependent entirely on the feelings, whereas love is a willed giving and caring, often with, but not dependent on, loving feelings. Man is born with both the equipment required for sex and the potential to love but he must acquire the goodwill and virtue to integrate his sex into his life of love, and so to be a better person himself and contribute to the personal growth of the one he loves.

Love is bigger even than death. Death never ends true love, and this makes it possible for men to die in peace. Those who love through death discover in subsequent love not the fickle replacement of a dead love but an enrichment of life made possible by an earlier love. Sex, on the other hand, barely endures through the emotional *now*.

Those who insist that man is a man only if he copulates, make manhood's qualifications pretty meagre. The man who does not love, whether he copulates or not, is much less a man. Sexual activity in itself does not express personal interest, understanding, companionship, mutual tolerance, support or inspiration, all qualities surpassing the purely sexual potential. Although the spirituality of sex is lost in removing sex from love, the humanity of sex is lost by removing love from sex. The more indispensable the sexual union the less vital the personal union, though the love bond is stronger because of the happily accepted sexual polarity. No deep friendship can exist when the sexual dimension is ignored, but it also doesn't exist when a relationship is purely sexual. Sex, which is personally destructive as a dominating force, reaches its perfection in the love-dominated person. People whose communication is limited to sexual intercourse soon have little in common and nothing to say to each other. The blind acceptance that sex is bigger than the person makes love impossible. Those who cannot wait until marriage to share their sexual lives, are writing off the loving life on which a happy marriage depends. Sex, which can contribute much to love, is never allowed to deprive wise or good people of the love which gives the meaning to sex, in fact, its humanity.

Love must be learned, it does not come automatically, however natural it is to man. Love certainly can be taught – in fact, deserves full status as a science, something to be studied, learned, understood and done. As one can be taught, though not made, to think, one can be taught, though not made, to love. But the power to love is in every human being and the best of teachers should be trained and provided to teach love, because the future of man depends, under God, entirely on the exercise of his power to love.

CHAPTER NINE

The High Cost of Unloving

The man who rejects his tremendous potential for happiness in loving must experience the terrible consequences of unloving. They are as clear as they are unpleasant. Addictions, crime, violence, hate and war on a scale not dreamed of, made inconceivably horrendous by advanced technology, rejecting all restraints by or direction from love, are the immediate ones. Man's intelligence is a disaster when he refuses to be good. However, the obvious cost of unloving, in the affluent society, is the loneliness so evident everywhere.

Loneliness is a long-lasting, devastating experience which everyone dreads, but few do much about. Man has moved so intelligently into less serious problems that it is beyond belief that he does so little about this one. The same diligent effort he has undertaken so often, applied to loneliness, would quickly bring the cure. The antidote for loneliness is loving. Not in being loved, but in positively loving others! In loving, man quickly discovers the cure for all psychosomatic disorders, the power he has to put his mind on someone other than himself. Loneliness is only a symptom of a malfunctioning will, and can be remedied by understanding love and acquiring the discipline, the virtue, to love. The poor, downtrodden, hungry and seriously ill do not feel loneliness much because of the more urgent and immediate pressures on them. The full impact of loneliness is felt predominantly by the materially successful, the affluent, who are aware of having everything except what matters most, love. Worldly success comes to most people through their ability and willingness to exploit others, the very process which breeds loneliness. It is being unloving rather than being unloved which causes loneliness.

Love is the power to invest oneself in others, in people rather than in things. Few of those so anxious to get, receive, have or possess are willing to lift a finger to love, because love has such low priority in their lust for power or for material things. Achievers worship success, almost purely material in their eyes. Having met the requirements of an academic-oriented society, they simply do not believe in a love they made no time for, which could only be an obstacle to their getting ahead. Love's magic escapes them until it is too late. Filled with the frustrations inseparable from success, and the contempt they have for those they have so easily exploited, idols in the midst of worshippers of the material, they are doomed to enjoy only a purchased love. They are victims of every kind of psychosomatic disease (their bodies have been so carefully cared for while their souls were starved); their doctors live off their illnesses. Hospitals are their houses of prostitution where they pay grudgingly for the purchased love to which they are addicted. Their psychiatrists and counselors are their fantasy lovers; the shallow, porcelain-cold, casual kiss of greeting at a door the warmest affection in their lives. When they cannot have whatever they want, they suffer withdrawal symptoms, emotional tantrums of one kind or another. Their power to love is cut off by their irresistible desire to be loved for what they are, even when they are obviously nothing. They die by inches of the cancer of addiction to themselves. The fulfilment in loving escapes them completely; their lifelong habit of dishonesty has cut them off, long ago, from the honest who alone could love them. As long as the eternal question is "What is in it for me?" the answer must inevitably remain, "Nothing, of course." Nothing is always the return on an investment never made.

The high cost of unloving, almost beyond reckoning, begins with the refusal to use one's basic capacity for real interest in others. That unused power inevitably turns to resentment, hate and corruption. The mercenary preoccupation of the news media with sex, crime, violence and corruption illustrates the ease with which genuine interest in others becomes morbid curiosity, shows how the exploitation of the misdeeds and misfortunes of others stimulates the sick delight in the unloving man who relishes the degrading exposure of the sins and weaknesses of his brother, as he gloats with feelings of relief and superiority. Such people all but demand, and the press goes to endless lengths to provide, the gory details of their neighbours' most revolting misadventures. The fantastic appetite for gossip, intrigue, character assassination, and the reduction of the high and mighty to less than life size, is indisputable evidence of interest perverted. People who would not develop the interest which in the beginning was genuine and efficacious, and could have led to love, everywhere excuse the worst in themselves by piously pointing to those who are more wicked than they. Those who, in their greed for riches and power, exploit the greed and corruption of the poor, who deplore the costs to themselves of a just society, pay vastly more for the protection of a tyranny dedicated to containing anarchy, to carrying on business as usual.

The honest, loving man contends with himself squarely and courageously. The dishonest, unloving man blames everyone else for his troubles, which multiply in direct proportion to his frustrations. History is a scathing record of the untapped potential for love flooding into destructive channels. The sordid record of hate makes it difficult to believe that the power of love is really greater. Hate is the alternative to love. It is the active refusal to respond to, and embrace, the good, ending in a determined effort to destroy the good. Real power is in the hands only of those who love or hate. The masses, in varying stages of indifference, bore themselves to death as addicts in pursuit of pleasure, or flight from pain, living on the fringes of love or hate, while the lovers and the haters make the future. War, mass hate, would seem to be reason enough to persuade anyone to love, yet peace has generally meant to the unloving masses merely the opportune leisure to resume their unimpeded exploitation of others. Protests against war are patently false when the protesters are not prepared to love. They are generally protesting only the interruption of their pleasures. Typically the unloving man looks for an easier road to peace than by confronting the truth which love makes possible. He wants to have his cake and eat it too. He will fight the man who takes him from the vomit of his choice.

The unloving man constantly runs through the litany of devils which make him unhappy – the establishment, the economic system, cultural heritage, skin pigment, unequal treaties, power blocs, the military-industrial complex, everything but himself. He screams, "Make love, not war," a beautiful slogan for those really prepared to love, but completely phoney when mouthed by those replacing the mass exploitation of war with the personal exploitation of irresponsible sex. To love, one must at least be winning the battle for possession of oneself, one must have acquired at least sufficient discipline to equate the good of another with one's own.

Crime is one man's war on himself, his neighbour and society. It is one man blowing his personal integrity for thirty pieces of silver. Gangsters, rioters, mobs, anarchists signify a sick society unequal to loving. Hate breeds hate. Violence, however understandable and seemingly commendable, merely replaces one tyranny with another. Genuine freedom is possible only where there is genuine love. Emerging races or nations simply pass from the jungle of ignorance to the jungle of exploitation, simply surrender one form of slavery for another, unless they weld loving to their learning and technology.

Every form of pollution is increased evidence of the high cost of unloving, the perverse destruction of the things man should love most and conserve. The lover alone accuses himself first and sees unloving as, essentially, man's pollution of himself. A little humour, which every unloving person lacks, would reveal the ridiculous stance of the man railing against air pollution as he stands censoriously glaring at an industrial smokestack, with a cigarette in his hand. Addicts can remain addicts only as long as they deny the obvious pollution of themselves by their own addictions. Man has little respect for nature when he has none for himself, when he blindly lays waste his fantastic power to love. His power to control nature is a bad joke if he will not control himself; true birth control surely must be seen first as self-control. Unloving is the rejection of personal discipline.

Emotional domination, the basis of addiction, must be added to the cost of unloving. The enlightened discernment and disciplined good judgment coming from love enable one to treat one's fellow man properly regardless of one's feelings. Great lovers can treat enemies with justice and decency. They alone can bring peace to the world, which prays for peace in vain unless it also loves. Emotionally dominated people can neither listen nor ponder. Easily aroused, they are generally in turmoil or complete withdrawal. Insecure, easily threatened and frightened, they react immediately to what is filtered through their overrriding emotions before they can even try to understand its real significance. The material of the senses is distorted by their twisted emotions, sending out alarms which create panic. They never really communicate. Their dialogues are "duologues" – two people talking, neither listening. For them love means the desire to possess; understanding means agreement; helping another means getting their own way; raising their children well means fulfilling themselves. Flattery is truth for them and jealousy the highest form of flattery. Their loveless marriages and hopeless homes are part of the high cost of unloving which, through emotional inflation, spawns the crippled tyrants who hate so well, and the cop-out parasites of society.

All addiction – to food or drink, to money, power, sex, or drugs – is slavery to self, man defaulting completely in the face of unpleasant reality. The addict with sufficient honesty to blame himself for his addiction is half cured. There is some hope that, despite every bad influence in his life – derelict parents, bad companions, poverty and suffering – he has the secret of happiness in his own power to love. The most stupid thing man can do is blame God and religion rather than himself for the strife and turmoil existing everywhere in the world, and use this excuse for seeking the hopeless shelter of addiction. The greatest hypocrites are the myopic scientists claiming utter objectivity in their search for truth, while rejecting the God of truth, beauty and goodness. Only the sick and selfish could smugly close their eyes to the human wreckage from pleasure addiction and the emotional binge which their "objective norms" have strewn around, more painfully obvious than the ruins of all the wars.

CHAPTER TEN

The Loving Life

The loving life is man at his best, so relating to others that he shares with them, to the fullest extent, all that he is and has. Before anyone loves deeply, he must accept man's inherent power to love; he must believe that God endowed man with such a potential. Belief in one's fellow man, which is the basis of love, lies in the conviction that however undeveloped, that power is there awaiting awakening by the loving of others. Those who refuse to accept this inherent power, and the obligation of using it for the development and growth of their fellow men, will use their own power to love in exploiting others for pleasure or other self-oriented purposes.

'My loving life begins when I learn to take an interest in each and every person I come in contact with, and my potential to love develops accordingly as I allow myself to be absorbed and fulfilled in those loving associations. I do not learn to love by singling out one person who interests or attracts me because that person represents something I need or want. Rather, in going out to all others around me according to *their* needs,' I discover any number of interesting people who respond to my interest and from among these I become aware of someone of such truth and beauty that a deeper relationship develops which is distinguished by its diffusive goodness. Out of a broad unselective experience of society come the deep, loving personal relationships characteristic of the loving life at its best, its most fruitful, its summit.

My loving interest is clearly shown by being what I can be to others and doing what I can do for others according to their needs, and to the opportunities provided and the resources available. I do not put people into my debt, nor do I create a personality cult. My interest is not selective or discriminatory, but given where necessary and possible. However casual it may be – and it always begins casually – it is always personal and genuine, rather than vague and contrived. My interest is restricted neither to equals, to inferiors, nor to superiors, but extends to all. It has the faculty of, and facility in, establishing a working equality with negligible sense of obligation or indebtedness, but a great sense of privilege. It is gracious rather than bountiful.

Man's survival depends on love to eliminate the exploitation passing for love in the lives of so many people. Love makes learning meaningful. Lacking love, academic learning must be oriented to pride, greed and self. Education has given man so many things he enjoys. However, he will lose them unless he shares them. The efficacious theology of affluence and sharing can show new nations that education without love is an avoidable disaster for man.

Prosperity has nothing but disillusionment to offer materialists, who see less and less to struggle for. As affluent America has grown richer and better fed, clothed and housed, she has become more corrupt, lazy, uninterested and selfish. People need to share their good things with others in love. Sharing offers something as essential to the benefactor as to the beneficiary. For much too long man's acknowledged needs have been material and physical, rather than spiritual and personal. Whoever dreamed up the delusion that the gospel cannot be preached to people with empty stomachs, obviously never tried to preach the gospel to people with full stomachs, whose fatty tissue so conveniently plugs their ears, insulating them from the truth. The poor and hungry people listen to the gospel because God is their only hope. They are too painfully aware that their fellow man could hardly care less about them. People with available resources seldom live with an awareness of their dependence on God; people who are physically comfortable tend to forget the spiritual. And love is spiritual, it is a power, an intangible, impressive both in what it is and in what it does. Love eludes those who are more impressed by what they have than by what they are.

The loving life is a whole person, aware of his dignity, worth and responsibility, living equally with his fellow man. The power to love enables a man to rise above his personal needs, which he readily equates with those of others and sacrifices for the common good. He achieves this life when he accepts that people are more important than things. Man gives many years of his early life to academic studies because his material progress requires it. He gives precious little time or thought to loving because he understands his physical well-being so much better than he appreciates growth as a person. Hopefully, as he now surveys the human wreckage around him, the mounting evidence of chronic unhappiness everywhere in the highly developed nations, he may be moved by the calamitous effects of unloving, the personal emptiness of his life, to set earnestly about the task of loving. The desperate need of the civilized world for the loving redemption of its technology is daily more apparent. The world's enthusiasm for loving must, at least, equal its enthusiasm for learning. The most primitive emerging nations now willingly budget for the education of their people because their proper development depends on it. They must understand and avoid the mistake of the industrial giants in letting love lag so far behind learning that progress is neutralized by unhappiness. The Church, which in the Western world pioneered so effectively in academic learning, must now turn its full attention and efforts to loving, the basic Christian commitment.

To achieve the loving life, man must accept that to remain unloving is to remain half developed, only half human. Not the unloved, but the unloving, fails as a person. How else explain the numbers of lonely people living in wealth? People with every material comfort remain desperate for fulfilment, for meaning in their still empty lives. They have tried every substitute for love – money, sex, prestige, drugs, and even the last desperate answer of all, the ultimate cop-out – suicide. How obviously only love is missing! How ridiculous not to give it a try! However poetical or ideal it sounds, the "I-thou" loving relationship is the reason for man's deep joy and happiness, his essential growth as a person. The "I-thou" loving relationship preserves man from addictions, to self, sex, drugs, food, drink and superstition. It liberates him from fear of pain, sorrow and sickness. Man prefers many things before love only because he is stupid or sick. So monstrous is his ego that he prefers his own judgment to God's, which is what sin is about. To avoid the calamity of unloving, man need only ask someone who has deeply loved whether love was wasted, regretted, or in any way a source of unhappiness. The answer would be clear enough. Unfortunately, each man has to learn for himself. The difference between real love and its many cheap imitations is in the certain, deep and lasting happiness that real love assures.

Man wants to love. The desire to love is built into him; love is an essential function for him. It is the most personal thing in his life. It cannot be done for him. He cannot be made to love. He has to choose, to will to do it. The loving life, however, is beyond one who confuses fulfilment with reward. Man is fulfilled when he functions as a man, that is, when he loves. He is rewarded when he is loved, which is something which can depend only indirectly on him, and for which he cannot be responsible. The truly loving person cannot be lured into loving by rewards, because he knows his fulfilment lies in his own positive loving. Among the immediate fruits of the loving life are true friendship, genuine community spirit, honest affection, meaningful courtship. These things are generated by people whose security and deep peace enable their love to manifest itself, without reserve, in genuine and efficacious interest in others.

All the above effects sound like tired clichés. They have great meaning, and yet convey an inescapable triteness which does not communicate their significance. Still, one can only try to express the rich meaning of those words, however threadbare their abuse has made them. Man is a social animal, so friendship is vital. Yet, the larger the number of friends claimed, the less the word friendship really means. Most people are so anxious to prove their irresistibility that they speak of the most casual acquaintances as friends. Realists speak of real friends in ones or twos. Anything more and they really mean community, a mutually interested and motivated group, not primarily friends. A real friend will immediately, at serious inconvenience to himself, willingly assist his friend in difficulty, not once or twice but as often as necessary, at any time. A friend is one with whom a person can be open, unafraid of exposure or rejection – in other words, secure.

The outstanding factor in friendship is the ability to communicate. To communicate one must be understanding, have some very real conviction, have awareness of and interest in others, and believe that one can open not one's body, but one's deepest self, to the other. Love makes the inevitable risk acceptable. The test of friendship between male and female is the love that outweighs sex, possessions, position or any emotional domination. To put it simply, friendship gives top priority to the good of the friend.

Community is the magic word. Yet only people who actually love can generate community. Community is not something one lives on but something one contributes to. Community is not built from crumbling bricks. It is totally defeated by people wanting privileges without accepting obligations, people who will not pay the bills. In real community the love of the strong sparks the weak to make them contributors; it raises them to life as only the miracle of love can. Community is not a group of parasites but an association of people of some goodwill, loving people. Unloving people drain community of its vitality. The corporate group gets hope from the resources of the group.

The bond between the members is love or it is delusion. The idea that members can be compelled rather than inspired to measure up is ridiculous.

The place of affection in the loving life is specific, and important. The necessity and role of affection should not be lightly overlooked or dismissed. Affection is like money; it has a real value which few use well. It can provide for or corrupt, assist or seduce. Needless to say, it is honest affection that is meant. Honest affection is the deliberate manifestation of feelings in a responsible relationship of true love, understood correctly by both persons in the relationship, never threatening but always contributing to its growth. It is as wrong to deprive loved ones of honest affection as it is to express dishonest affection. Genuine affection has been too generally suppressed because too much dishonest affection is too easily expressed. The manner and degree of the affection expressed depend entirely on the good of the people involved. That is to say, it is always given and received in the context of one's commitments and intentions. For example, the affection of married people is extended to others within the limits of their marriage commitment; parents are not incestuous; celibate affection is not genitally geared. True affection is never an occasion of hardship, confusion or serious emotional upset to anyone involved. Affection can be a nod, a smile, or a knowing look and may go on to a holding of hands, a hug, a kiss or other endearment which has a real message of genuine loving interest but is never attempted seduction. In genuine loving relationships none of these actions need cause genital sex arousal, though, of course, they can be used for this purpose, or can be mistaken as being intended for this purpose. To say that such honest affection is impossible or wrong is merely to insist that love is impossible.

Because of the traditional suspicion of affection it can be very disconcerting to the good people best qualified to give and receive it. This is mainly because of the accompanying sexual emotions which, if understood, are very helpful in gauging the acceptable intensity of its expression. These feelings, in themselves, are never reason to suppress affection. Affection shown should truly represent and be understood for what it is – the manifestation of a special, personal, loving relationship. The secondary sexual element in all affection is normal and healthy. However, the honest affection of mature people is of a personal, not a sexual, significance. It never has primary sexual overtones. Thus, honest affection inevitably results in both people being better people, more relaxed, secure, open to, and understanding of each other, more interested in, useful and available to others. Good people who have no one with whom to be themselves, or to whom they can reveal themselves, tend to crack up.

In contrast, affection which results in sexual frustration, exclusiveness, possessiveness (not in feelings only but in fact), lessening of dedication and chronic discontent with life, all characteristics of emotionally dominated people – such affection is always dishonest. Inadequate people are devastated by feigned affection simulating exclusive friendship. They generally misinterpret even the affection displayed as routine common courtesy. Misused affection leaves scars as deep as brutality; it makes emotional cripples. Honest affection is displayed in attitude, interest, word and action; it is stimulated by friendship, the ability of friends to communicate and understand, and other similar factors.

Courtship is a circumstance of special love and friendship. There is then a specific relationship in which both people honestly expect marriage to eventuate. There is both more reason for expressed affection, and a much greater danger of self-deception and dishonesty. The great tendency and danger is to justify the present manifestations of affection by an uncertain future relationship which simply cannot justify them, instead of being sure that they are restricted to the realities of the relationship present here and now. The very honesty which rejects the exploitation so understandable in courtship is the quality which indicates responsible maturity and real hope of love in the possible future relationship. Courtship is undeniably the greatest opportunity to learn the discipline required by love in a happy marriage, *e.g.*, the discipline required for fidelity, good management, responsible parenthood. It foresees almost every difficulty to be encountered in marriage, and should be a time of deep understanding and thoughtful concern, rather than of wishful thinking and mirages.

True interest in the welfare of the loved permits loving people to enjoy courtships, and prevents those courtships from being traumas of emotional desire and possessiveness, in which the lust for sexual fulfilment obliterates all real hope of personal relationship.

The sexual intercourse which is of such high excitement in courtship almost inevitably becomes a bore in marriage. Only interesting people can keep sex from becoming a bore. Love makes courtship a process of personal discovery quite within the capability of those genuinely interested in others, though quite beyond those who can't face themselves, let alone expose themselves to the discerning scrutiny of another. Love is the power not to be sidetracked in courtship by any lesser dimension than the personal, so that the courtship actually leads to a marriage in which the sexual sharing is enjoyed in the context of the personal love. Marriage should take place between people already loving, who have successfully negotiated the risks in learning to love. To make modern courtship an emotional standoff of immature people in a highly explosive situation is to assure the destruction of marriage as an institution. The loving life equips people for responsible courtship, which is true courtship rather than trial marriage, or more correctly, trial sex. When the interest of people in each other peaks in a sex-oriented courtship, a tragic marriage generally follows in which one or both parties soon abandon any honest effort to love.

CHAPTER ELEVEN

The Loving Married Life

Marriage ought to represent an irrevocable, exclusive, deep personal commitment to another for life, by one who considers himself obligated without recourse to contribute everything within his power to the growth and development of the other person. The problem marriage is the one in which the immature seek fulfilment in the love they want to receive and the rewards they expect to get. Mature people are ready for marriage, ready to give. One is sexually mature at twelve or fourteen years of age, but emotionally mature only when sex has been integrated into loving, that is, when one is capable of the deep, loving relationship required by marriage. This can be said only of those who have a valid set of values, including the spiritual ones. Marriage should be reserved to people who do love. One must not wait for marriage to learn to love. It was possible to do that in the past, when the institution was supported by so many cultural props not present in modern urban living. It is virtually impossible today.

The loving marriage is the most complete person-to-person relationship. But few people who have not learned to love before marriage do so after. When the excitement of infatuation and sex fulfilment dies down and the novelty of both wears off, very little relationship between the people is discovered. Marriage does offer loving people a better opportunity for a deeper relationship than simple friendship because it includes the full use of the sexual dimension with a valid exclusiveness and fuller union. However the use people make of that opportunity depends entirely on the degree to which they are truly loving, which has precious little to do with marriage in itself. Loving people so relate in marriage as to pool their resources in common creative interests. They have, when truly loving, such security that the good of others never threatens their own. From the strength of their unthreatened love they share themselves with others, primarily their children. And children are essential to a loving marriage. To a loving couple a childless marriage is a frustration, to be solved by adoption or investment of themselves in the equivalent of a family.

A loving marriage is the human completion of man in both the sexual and personal senses. It is the actual full equation of the good of a special person with one's own. This unfortunately is not true of most marriages, not through any defect in the institution, but through the fault of the people. Being a social animal, man not only needs others, but procreates them through his closest personal association in love – marriage. Because man's need of others is much more personal than sexual, love in marriage is far more important than sex. Sex in marriage works best in the loving production of people, that is in the loving production of each other, for each other. The "I-thou" relationship so fundamentally needed by man can produce the kind of society in which man is most fully at home. In such a society man's primary and most vital relationship is not mere physical coupling but a union of whole people at their very mature best.

When marriage means love, rather than a licence to copulate, its preservation as an institution will be assured. Man has come a long way from the days when love in marriage was a luxury and children a necessity. With progress in science man has more control of his material destiny, and must develop the love required for his fulfilment as a human being. Love is now necessary for a happy marriage.

Children today seldom contribute to the material security or physical comfort of parents, but, on the contrary, are to a large extent a discomfort, a burden and responsibility, calling for greater parental love and dedication. Previously, they were required to help with the material establishment of the family and provide its food and protection, and as replacements for those taken by death and sickness and other then unavoidable disasters. Although pensions and insurance cannot replace children as emotional security in old age, they have replaced them as financial security.

One no longer has to raise six children so that two will survive adolescence, and one of those willingly support the parents in their old age. Since parents now not only survive, but survive much longer, they provide for their own old age. Thus there is pressure to have fewer children and provide better for themselves. Parents now must mean more to each other.

Modern parents outlive their basic responsibility to their children, and thus parents who were busily occupied with children for many years generally find themselves alone with each other when the children are established on their own. They surprisingly discover that they hardly know each other. In their concern and busyness about the children they never developed a personal relationship and so find themselves virtual strangers, often both uninterested and uninteresting. When the love so vital in marriage today is needed most, it simply does not exist because there has been no concerted effort to achieve it.

The public, which took for granted an automatic love relationship in marriage, must now realize that such a relationship must be studied and worked at if it is to exist. Love is not always easy or pleasurable but it is always possible. Freer than he ever was from all but the sexual pressure to marry, man must accept that sexual attraction is the poorest basis on which to build a marriage. The sexual relationship is not necessarily a loving one and, in itself, seldom leads to love. Scientists can present and explain the purely mechanical aspects of the genital function and still do nothing for love, and therefore nothing really vital to help unhappy marriages. People who have little to say to each other before marriage will find, after a very few years of marriage with few children or none, that they still have nothing to say to each other and sex itself has become a dull bore. There is no relationship at all. One should only marry one with whom it is joy to share ideas, thoughts and plans, and who is capable of a relationship far exceeding the sexual.

Negatively sex-dominated moralists have left a legacy of misguided notions of both lust and love. The mere having of children was made a virtue, whether they were conceived, born and raised in love or in negligence. Lust is as destructive of love in marriage as out of it. In the loving marriage there is certainly the power to direct sex to the thoughtful, loving conception of children. Those who will not control their sex appetites are poor lovers and even poorer parents, simply because they are incapable of the concern for others which is love.

Children ought never to be the accidental result of the uncontrolled passion of parents. Though deeply loving people do generally want the children they conceive, few accept that they need only have the children they want, or that the sexual function can be directed to that end simply because it is under the same controls as any of man's powers, which are less than himself. The conception of children should be considered a privilege. Children are new people to be brought, by loving parents, into a world critically short of people willing to share their love with others. Certainly, the intricate planning, fantastic calculations and incredible costs of space exploration invalidate the contention that the thoughtful, loving conception of children by man is too difficult a challenge. But this contention must persist as long as people prefer the pleasure of sex to its purpose, on which the pleasure is based. The progress of man, in love as in all things, depends on the dedicated goodness of the few who inspire its miracles.

The primary, but by no means exclusive, purpose of sex is the loving production of a family. Marriage is an obstacle to the sterile pseudo-love between people with no interest whatever in fruit from their love. The loving marriage must be fruitful in children because real love is of its essence creative. Any partner is eternally grateful to a deceased spouse who thoughtfully left the living with an inheritance of happy memories and a fruitful love. Money is a disappointing substitute for the living legacy of loving children witnessing the love that was. They can be provided only by people whose relationship is deeper than money or possessions, whose lives are lived in mutual interest and the loving service of a happy marriage, in a home made joyful and alive with loving people. In a culture in which this concept becomes obsolete, marriage must lose its meaning and become merely a licence for people to cohabitate in respectable sterility. Marriage, for far too many people, is a legal service to assure equitable distribution of the spoils on dissolution of a contract, the duration of which is as predictable as the people signing it.

The drug addiction currently laying waste the human resources of the affluent society is merely the beginning of the harvest of unhappiness being reaped in the unloved children of a sick society. Children conceived and born unloved are just as crippled as the thalidomide babies of the recent drug scandal. When they are reared in neglect, the future of such children is indeed bleak. The social philosophers who, in typical oversimplification, recommend contraceptives to insure against unloved babies contribute nothing to the development of loving people. However accepted, rationalized or justified, the use of contraceptives does nothing to bring loving within the reach of man. They are, at best, the lesser of evils. No one enjoys using them. When love is properly understood children can be conceived, born and reared in love, rather than as an accident of sexual indulgence or through complete indifference to the responsibility of parenthood.

It is ridiculous to think that sexually indulgent, pleasure-oriented people can suddenly become loving and self-sacrificing when they decide that they are ready to conceive and bear a child. Such people conceive their children as projections of their own egos, and seldom respect the person or the rights of the children themselves, as the legalization of abortion so clearly indicates. Those people who promote abortion, rejecting the full rights of the foetus, will not respect the personal rights of the newborn infants either, but will use them for their own satisfaction. To "feel" the need for children is not sufficient reason for conceiving them without the will to love them. Our affluent, emotionally crippled world is full of children prostituted to the projected ambitions of parents, who, unable to inspire the respect of their children, bribe them for it with indulgences. Parents who bribe their children for affection are oblivious to the proper growth and development of the children, which requires parental unwillingness to spoil them.

The current shortsightedness of the abortion solution to unwanted children is incredible in civilized society. Hardly a voice is heard to question the sexual irresponsibility creating the pregnancy. It is indeed an Alice-in-Wonderland society which will respect "No Parking" signs, support civil rights, and deplore child massacres in wartime and poverty and hunger in the underdeveloped nations, while its youngest citizens (foetuses of less than twenty weeks) are flushed down hospital drains, too young to hire a lawyer or appeal to the United Nations, a mere ten weeks from the full protection of the law. Criminals and hoodlums indeed fare better in that society.

Premarital intercourse is probably no more damaging than being raised in a puritan, antisexual atmosphere which implies that sex is an unnatural, uncontrollable monster. But despite the permissive extravagance of behavioural scientists, there is no solid evidence that premarital intercourse has any inherent value. In fact, the evidence is against anticipating marital privileges without assuming marriage obligations, if one wishes to be happy. Love cannot be bought with a credit card. However, it should surprise no one that the society which rejects almost all restraint on any other pleasurable emotion, also rejects sexual restraint. When "doing your thing" is stupidly identified with doing as you feel like doing, rather than with making every effort to reach your potential as a human being, few are willing to admit that controlling one's sexual appetites is at least possible, and even more necessary than controlling one's temper. Marriage is no remedy for uncontrollable sexual desires, which are not always or easily satisfied in marriage. Uncontrolled urges wreck any relationship, and marriage tolerates few delusions about sex. The miracle of self-control, so essential to love, does not descend on the undisciplined person by the fact of marriage. A successful married life requires sexual discipline as much as success in business requires work discipline. It should be noted that those who make discipline easy by eliminating normal sexual emotions from their lives form the harmful habit of avoiding other unpleasant realities, and make it almost impossible to relate to others realistically as love requires.

The worthwhile sexual relationship in marriage is experienced in the worthwhile personal relationship. The easily aroused man may be momentarily stimulating but he is impossible to live with, and marriage is living together in love. The married couple should be first of all good friends. Incredible as it seems, any number of well educated, materially successful, physically attractive adults find themselves unable to discuss many aspects of their personal lives with their spouses. The idea that people who share the same bed for years, and appear easily before each other in their physical nakedness, will automatically appear easily before each other in the naked intimacy of their emotional and personal lives in quite erroneous. Only those who have the full acceptance of the other in love can do this, since love alone creates enough security to risk misunderstanding. Too many are content to let their marriage stagnate in a relatively pleasant sexual relationship often personally meaningless. Sex plays an exaggerated role in their lives because they are afraid to communicate more than can be disguised with a passionate kiss; they are afraid of any penetration deeper than that of sexual intercourse. Awareness of another as a body is in no way awareness of another as a person. The delightful security of those whose relationship can surely survive misunderstandings is the basis for communication. The depth of love in any marriage can be correctly gauged by the actual communication between the parties.

Loving marriage is the union of people who understand each other. Generally troubled marriages are between immature, insecure people who primarily "feel" they love each other but admittedly do not understand each other, have made little or no studied effort to understand each other, and generally do not have a clue as to what understanding involves, let alone the courage or purpose to undertake it. They speak without conversing, and "communication" means only reassurance for themselves, rather than understanding of the other. For insecure people, understanding always means agreement, rather than awareness of how the other person thinks and feels regardless of agreement or disagreement. Understanding of another comes with the eagerness to hear and the desire to ponder, which is beyond people who talk all the time, who fear to listen and dread thinking because they cannot risk disillusionment. Such people may be legally married but they are not lovingly married; they are capable of sharing their bodies in intercourse but not their personhood in understanding. Acceptance in so many marriages depends on the degree to which the couple do not know each other, or worse, the degree to which they are able to deceive each other. So many of them quite truthfully say, "I could never tell my wife or my husband that," expressing exactly the very limited dimensions of their love.

Love cannot be expected to mature in a marriage in which neither party has the self-respect, or desire, to continue growing as a person. The allure of most wives after the second child or a few years of marriage is about equal to the chivalry of their husbands. Being bored to death is a hard way to die, and boredom is the fate of married people refusing to make themselves interesting as people, and inspiring to their partners. Surely the job of being personally attractive is worthy of as much effort as the job of being physically attractive. Those whose understanding and use of beauty aids is restricted to commercial products and plastic surgery, have no appreciation of genuine personal beauty, or the virtues which keep the heart young and love fresh. A constant growth in goodness and deepening of integrity by both people make marriage a wonderful relationship and give the partners a continuing sense of privilege.

External compulsion to persist in a marriage in which there is no relationship between the people, or when it is realized that there was no real marriage in the first place, has caused thoughtful people to rebel against an irrevocable decision being made, in a highly emotional situation under considerable sexual compulsion, to enter a relationship with so many more dimensions than sex. The obvious, and too easy, answer is trial marriage with contraceptives. Although this cop-out appals because of its unrealism, any mistake seems preferable to emotionally crippled children born of a meaningless union which is farcically maintained because public morality or public order apparently demands it. The answer surely is not to make a farce out of marriage but to insist that people qualify for marriage by learning to love.

The unloving married relationship exists because the people in it will not love. They have the power to do so, if they wish to use it. Their problem is like that of the alcoholic. They must first recognize the problem, admit it and then do what has to be done – learn to love. Almost any marriage can be made to work if the parties have the goodwill basic to the loving relationship. The marriage in which love has "died" can be resurrected if the parties will learn to love instead of running away to begin the same disappointing process with other partners as immature as themselves. It takes honesty and courage to see and admit the loveless marriage, but that same honesty and courage make love possible between those willing to seek help from good friends or competent counselors with valid convictions about love, personal relationships and marriage.

Counselors, like psychiatrists, are a mixed bag. Their competence demands the conviction that love directs sex to the production of the loving family in which happily married people are deeply invested, and of which they are very protective. The prophets of the new morality rightly insist that functional sex and the preservation of the species do not require marriage. However, love and the development of the human potential to love, do. Marriage is merely the commitment of those sufficiently loving to direct their lives through sex to the personal union which welcomes children and supplies the milieu for their basic emotional health. Counselors who do not see marriage as the commitment underlying the secure atmosphere in which lovers can grow personally are more a menace than a help. Such counselors lack the artistic imagination to explain the value of stable marriage in the development of the partners as people.

Learning to love requires imagination, the ability and eagerness to see ahead and plan for the future with enough flexibility to include the wishes and aspirations of another person. The imagination can present an authentic picture of the happy loving marriage, the qualities to develop in oneself and to seek in one's partner, the joys to be expected in companionship and sharing, the goodwill and personal costs they require. The lack of imagination, or the poorly directed imagination, is largely responsible for the false picture of undiluted happiness which many young lovers accept without question as they go blithely into marriage. Their ultimate disillusionment in each other and in marriage could have been prevented by the studied application of the imagination to their prospective relationship, well before marriage. The imagination previews the realities of marriage and outlines the adequate personal preparation. The competent counselor does the same, if the imagination has not. But he himself must be convinced of the potential for love in everyone, and refuse to see personal failures as defects in the institution of marriage.

Marriage counselors are plagued with people lacking the imagination which makes understanding possible, and love a reality. Sex and its overrated pleasure, mistaken emphasis on minor factors in personal relating, can ultimately revolt both parties in a marriage. When one is all fired up for making love and the other completely enervated from a hopeless day at the office, or in the home, neither understanding the needs of the other, there is no place to go. Some imagination would make it plain that there are burdens to be disposed of, and understanding to be given and received, if the sharing of bodies is to truly represent the sharing of lives. People, capable of personal relationships, who begin by sharing their bodies in love can go on to deeper, mutual interest and genuine personal concern for the other. However, the union of bodies being so easy and superficially rewarding, most unions tend to stop there. If so, lack of imagination and interested effort to explore each other in depth bankrupt love before communication is ever established. After mutual sexual exploitation, the marriage is like a worked-out mine, leaving the exploiters to separate in their search for other fields to conquer.

The economic crises of marriage, which, counselors seem to agree, form about 30% of all marriage problems, require great imaginative understanding simply because the male and female approaches to the economy of home and family are so different. The understanding agreement required for the raising of the family also requires tremendous imaginative thought and disciplined planning, made possible by the foresight and vision flowing from a developed imagination. Evidence of the unimaginativeness of man lies in his unquestioning will to spend eighteen or twenty years of his life qualifying himself academically for a money-earning job to pay for his marriage and the raising of a family, while refusing to spend even a small part of that time learning to love, his very reason for existing. This will continue to be the situation as long as people refuse to see that the highest human fulfilment consists in loving, and that marriage is the ideal situation for the deepest interpersonal relationships.

Because marriage is usually dominated more by sex than by love, many are unhappy about its indissolubility. They consider that marriages ought to be considered valid only between contracting parties who are indeed genuinely loving people. These are the only people capable of such a commitment. Love is the essence of Christian marriage because love is what Christianity is all about, however forgotten or unnoticed that may be. As the unloving person can be Christian in name only, the loveless marriage can be Christian in form, but certainly not in substance. Divorce, however, by no means assures that a broken marriage will be followed by a happy one, unless by some miracle the people become loving in the meantime. Realistic canonical marriage legislation should permit only loving people to enter a relationship expected to endure. Certainly, those willing to study and develop the great human potential to love can make happy and lasting marriages. Unloving people are not eligible for Christian marriage. Education which was really Christian would make that clear. Love cannot be guaranteed in Christian marriage unless the marriage takes place between people who are first of all real Christians. There is nothing wrong with marriage as an institution which love cannot cure. To fail to love is not only to lack real faith and scoff at God, but it is to lack the very qualities which led to every notable human achievement. It surely is ridiculous to accept years of work as basic for education while expecting to "fall" into meaningful love.

Married love and celibate love are equally beautiful; both are much more alike than different, because love is a marvellous achievement inseparable from the happiness of man. Married love is that very image of God seen in those beautiful people, contentedly interdependent and independent after fifty years of marriage, capable of being and living alone because they are secure enough to give each other the glorious opportunity to love fully, freely. They are whole people presenting to each other nearly unlimited horizons for loving and giving. They share great understanding of love with celibates because they see love as God in their midst; dependent on God, they cannot see their love enduring if cut off from God, its source. They find it easy to believe in God and to accept immortality because the love they share is so obviously a spiritual and indestructible thing, originating in, and destined for, endurance in a spiritual and eternal sphere. Despite the inevitable deterioration of the body, love for them remains essentially ageless, young, fresh and expectant. They have no sense of their love dying, and accept death as something restricted to the body. They are the antithesis of loveless people who have as little to live for as to die for.

The difference between married and celibate loves is purely sexual. The common factor is love. In marriage only love keeps sex from taking the lover's mind away from the person of the loved one. In celibacy only love can put such emphasis on the person that sex cannot intrude on the relationship. The same degree of love which keeps sex in its place in marriage keeps sex in its place in celibacy. Without that love marriage and celibacy are equally meaningless charades.

CHAPTER TWELVE

The Loving Celibate (Single) Life

Perhaps the sexual aspect of morality has been stressed too much, to the detriment of justice, mercy and charity. Yet sexual morality has great meaning for most, and is, when genuine, admired even when not imitated. Most of us like people who are pure though not puritan, strong though not intolerant, gentle though not pushovers. For these, the chapters on celibacy have something to say.

Celibacy is under fire today, and persistent effort is being made to dismiss it as certainly unloving, if not humanly destructive. Its value is easily overlooked because of gross misunderstanding and misuse. I speak with some authority on celibacy and believe in it. However, one thing must be made clear before presenting my reasons for doing so. Celibacy must have little meaning for those who dismiss the realistic relationship between man and God which is true religion. But then, so must love. But for those who accept human love as a God-given power, celibacy is desirable in all premarital and extramarital relationships between man and woman. Many thoughtlessly conclude that since the celibate priesthood and religious life have been facts of Catholic life for centuries, priests have more obligation to chastity than other Christians. In reality, all single people have the obligation to celibate chastity until marriage. Then, married chastity limits genital sex to one's spouse – a severe restriction. Nothing so prepares a man for fidelity in marriage as fidelity to God before marriage. It is self-evident that one who does not respect God and what He stands for will not likely respect a spouse sufficiently to remain faithful to her.

Furthermore, though the only difference between the Christian celibate and the single Christian is the promise of one to be celibate for life, while the other promises it only until marriage, the qualities and virtues required by each are the same. Those are the qualities which make it possible to learn to love before marriage, and are the best assurance that there will be love in marriage. People who can control their sexual life before marriage do not have to learn something new in marriage, where it is not easily learned.

Again, there is, or has been, a tragic respect for the fact, rather than the virtue, of virginity. So now virginity is often being discarded altogether without realizing that in being rid of the ridiculous and irrelevant, something very precious is being cast aside with little understanding of its inherent worth. Physical virginity in itself represents no human value. An intact hymen is about as necessary as an unremoved appendix. Much has been made of virginity while virtually ignoring the fidelity to God and one's spouse which underlies chastity. This is the virginity which, as a high human achievement, promises much happiness to deeply loving people. It is rather ludicrous to remain virgin out of pure pride, while saints who lost their physical virginity lived for years afterwards in the state of moral virginity because of their love for God and fellow man. For some strange reason, physical virginity seems a desirable quality in the brides of so many egocentric men responsible to a large degree for the scarcity of virgins. This is, of course, typical of the double standard which mocks virtue while expecting happiness to come in some miraculous way after years of self-indulgence. However strange it is, few such men, even in the permissive society, are easily reconciled to the promiscuity of their wives or daughters.

For those who dismiss the idea, or fact, of God in human life, sex and love simply do not work for the happiness of man, on a permissive basis. No achievement esteemed by the professional world is the result of accident, indifference or anything but persistent, hard work, ideals, hopes and expectations.

The general Christian teachings about sex and love have come down through a celibate-dominated Church. While many good things came this way, hang-ups and problems were created by it also. If these are to be understood and avoided, then the mistakes that went into training celibates, as well as the mistakes in celibate living itself, must be clearly seen as such. Celibates are not more immune to error than others, and like everyone who undertakes a solemn obligation to do something difficult they tend to make the fulfilment of it as easy as possible. The effort to do just that led to the commonly held conviction that celibacy and human love are irreconcilable. They are, in fact, inseparable. The celibate teacher's attitude to sexual morality led to the erroneous conclusion by many that marriage was a second-rate institution for the weaker people unequal to the "virtue" required by celibacy. And this in spite of the obvious fact that many celibates voided their vows through weakness, while many married people reached a degree of virtue admittedly heroic. No husband and wife reach the high happiness of married life who do not share the virtues of the good celibate, whose love for each other has not reached such intensity that sexual abstinence, for good reason, is both possible and acceptable. Certainly, many difficulties and hang-ups of celibates in sexual matters were passed on to the Christian and his culture.

Celibacy is especially relevant, however, for the ever more numerous people who, for any number of reasons, remain single, either for a long time or for life. They, too, must love if they are to become fully human. They want to be good people, to maintain their self-respect and their integrity without being complete squares. They are anxious to learn to love. Then too, there are any number of divorced people, left to lead single lives, disenchanted with the romance of marriage and badly burned from the searing experience of rejection. Yet, somehow or other, they believe in personal love and all that it involves. Many of these people will remarry, but in the meantime, while they are learning to love, their lives will be, for all practical intents and purposes, celibate in almost everything but the lifetime commitment. However few they may be, they are not easily sucked in by the beautiful theories of permissive love which so obviously leave innumerable human wrecks in their wakes. They want to learn to really love, as single people, to relate in a personal way, which puts meaning in life and brings happiness.

Something special must be said of the single girl, liberated from almost all cultural ties to home and the sheltered life, competing for a living in the commercial world on a nearly equal basis with men. It is only in modern times that women have become the large working force that they are today in Western civilization. Years ago, many good young girls entered the convent because it was their only alternative to staying home with their mothers and fathers, being domestic slaves. After World War I the idea of women working in industry and commerce became acceptable. Now, few women are content to go from school to marriage and a home, nor are homes that easy to come by in modern urban life. Most want to qualify themselves for a second career, by spending some years single and self-supporting. Many do not want to be swingers, playing games because of the loneliness and misery of the big cities to which they escaped from the small-town background where their undoubted superiority made marriage with the local boys an unhappy prospect at best. They often find themselves unequal to the effort to persist in virtue, choosing a temporary affair with a married man, or some other single person also unprepared for the obligations of a marriage, rather than remaining alone and lonely in the anonymity of the termite life of high-rise urban living. For these, too, the principles governing celibate love have meaning and perhaps offer some help. At least they will know that there are alternatives to sexual orgies or devastating loneliness.

Loving relationships with good people are open to them if they learn that love need never cut off circulation to their brains, if they grasp how easily the emotions can be used to prompt the mind to preview the tragedy of stolen hours and usurped privileges in the Never-never Land of unreality, located one stop before the abortionist's office or the home for unwed mothers. It is incredible that history must repeat itself in broken hearts because so few learn that true love is never blind.

CHAPTER THIRTEEN

Loving Celibacy

Before anyone can commit himself to the celibate life he must be convinced that celibacy is essentially a loving life, and that he chooses to love in this way. Christ, who was celibate, left a single command; *to love*. Though ritual Christian worship is the Agape, the love-feast of the Eucharist, the actual worship is the daily loving life, genuine loving interest in this person here and now, in the flesh, through the Spirit of Love, in a willful, personal love. Such love is evidence of Christ's continuing presence in the world; by it all men can recognize His actual disciples. Love is the living expression of Christian faith to which the celibate dedicates his life. Otherwise celibacy is a delusion and a very unhappy way to live.

Obviously, then, true celibacy is full of meaning, a very positive way of life. Generations of Christian celibates, unfortunately, had it drummed into them that if they were "good priests or religious" they were everything. "Good" was defined with legal negatives so that they could, in some mysterious way, be considered loving without actually loving anyone. They were encouraged to be real men and women while completely ignoring sex and their positive sexuality. They succeeded, all too often, only in eliminating love, which is the one justification for celibacy. Much of the present temporary rejection of celibacy can be explained by this historic development of celibate life into the obligation to love no one but God alone. Such celibacy is as unchristian as it is unloving.

Christianity is not an establishment, structure or system, but a personal confrontation with the Truth, God, in the honest effort to love. Since Christianity is their profession, celibates should lead the way in loving Christ – the Way, the Truth and the Life, the expression of God in the world *in people*. Christian celibacy is essentially an act of faith in God, in His expressed Word, Jesus Christ, and in Christ's parting gift to men, the Spirit of Love who lives in people.

Where there is no actual loving there is no religion, no real relationship to God, and liturgical worship is an empty mockery. Genuine love is not emotional, possessive or exclusive, but willful, expansive and inclusive. There is room in the loving celibate's life for all to be loved, all in whom he must be interested, all with whom he must share himself. His love is very human and personal, not angelic nor purely spiritual; it is always for the good of the ones loved. His public worship of God is then the true expression of the life he is living.

Real love, so vital to celibacy, does not come easily, and for that reason fulfilled celibates are rare. Before it came to the apostles they had to be devastated by Christ's death on the cross as a criminal. They expected Him to avoid it; they wanted triumph and public acclaim for Him, and a share in it for themselves, of course. Their incredible joy on His reappearance after the resurrection was short-lived because He had told them before He died that He was soon to leave them again. "Still I must tell you the truth: it is for your own good that I am going because unless I go, the Advocate will not come to you," He said (John 16:7). Their reaction clearly showed their need for the Spirit of Love. Their concern was entirely for themselves, not for Him. They simply could not imagine that He was going away because it was best for them, because He loved them. They did not want to hear of His going. Before celibates can ever trust enough to love they have to learn, somehow or other, that God's ways are better, surer, always right, and that if He expects them to love He will help them. They must have deeper faith, not in themselves, but in Him.

Loving celibacy is active and effective interest by the personally secure whose preoccupation with self and with personal needs is minimal. The celibate's interest in others is more thoughtful and willful than is required for sex. His genuinely interested love and its responsibility mature him much as they do a husband or wife in a loving marriage, and lead to a relationship much broader and more fruitful than a sexual one. A deep involvement in the welfare of others stimulates creativity and provides absorbing happiness.

The celibate is essentially human, sex-endowed, equipped like the average man or woman to find sexual fulfilment. Man's fulfilment is normally achieved by doing all things well, including his God-given sexual life. Naturally, then, genuine celibates will be relatively few, but they will be people who forgo sex only to love better and more, whose sexual life is sacrificed – that is, made holy – by dedicating themselves to loving God and man through extraordinary service. Their sexual fulfilment will be compensated for by the more encompassing fulfilment of personal love. In this sense, celibacy cannot be called a normal state. Its explanation and justification are the high degree of loving involved in a deliberate choice of a way to love that is as demanding as a loving marriage, and possibly more personally fulfilling. Celibacy's motive is the imitation of the celibate life of Jesus Christ, dedicated to the utterly essential task of teaching love to a humanity threatening to destroy itself by unloving, by denying its very power to love, by letting itself be distracted from loving by sex, money, power, greed, and all the things diametrically opposed to the best development of men, things which block men's vision of God and usurp the place of God in their lives.

Comfortable bachelorhood or spinsterhood has only a superficial resemblance to Christian celibacy, in that the persons are unmarried. The comfortable bachelor priest quite logically replaces people in his life with things, prestige, power, the big rectory, the big car, the big table, the big bottle, the big wallet, the big colour TV. Little wonder, then, that he feels the need of a sexual partner, which is about all he lacks. After all, one does not feel the need of what one already has. If the comfortable bachelor priest does leave and get married, he remains a bachelor at heart, because his own comfort still has top priority in his life. For every priest who goes astray for a woman, ten have been seduced by the bottle and thirty by the wallet. Those who do not love are very easily seduced by many things. In contrast, the genuine celibate values things only in so far as they are useful in loving. Neither money, material possessions nor personal comforts are valued for themselves but as things to be shared gratefully, used without fear of loss or coveting the security they so falsely represent. Comfort and rest contribute to one's work and the glad service given those in need, the threatened, fearful, insecure and alienated.

Loveless celibacy produces cantankerous, small-minded people, prone to bickering jealousy, who constantly resent the friendships of others – an indictment of their own unloving. Well-meaning spiritual directors, often unknowingly, imposed loveless lives on normal people in the name of God – for example, by ordering penitents to avoid good relationships because the directors feared them dangerous. Few realized that their constant suspicion of mature religious in loving situations was merely the projection of their own suppressed sexual desires. Such celibacy is negative, cruel, even sadistic. It is certainly unchristian. To it can be attributed many a nervous breakdown which could have been easily avoided. The victims of loveless celibacy, wise enough to know that no one praises God through a nervous breakdown, are saved if they can turn to someone who loves them, whom they can trust, who sees through the false image of holiness they project. The genuine love of that person will send them back to their work more realistic, effective and dedicated than before, since real love never exploits the temporary dependence of the loved one, but rejoices in his strength and goodness.

Celibates should be living gospels, really Good News, reflecting the life of Jesus Christ and the loving relationships between Him and His closest friends, and the relationship between Joseph and Mary. Celibacy does not downgrade sex, or imply that its use in marriage need be less than beautiful, for sex as much as love is the work of God. Celibacy is one way of living a loving life, marriage is another. The best Christians are those who love well, whether celibate or married. People, not states of life, have the potential to love. But great love is not only within the potential of celibates, it is their professed goal. Their vow not to marry is a manifestation of an extraordinary, chosen way to love. Their God-centred, people-centred love is a delusion if their sexuality is not incorporated into their loving relationships. Unloving celibates have absolutely nothing to offer to so much of the world, that is living unfulfilled simply because it has not learned to love.

The celibacy of the immediate past has been largely dedicated to academic learning. Unfortunately, too many of the celibates have become trapped in the very esteem for education they so rightly encouraged in the world. Charity, originally, was behind the desire and effort of the Church to provide schooling for people who would otherwise never get it in the days before taxation provided public education. This charity drew great numbers of dedicated teaching celibates. However, as the standards of public school surpassed those of religious schools, the brighter celibates were sent on to achieve academic excellence in the sciences and languages, while the less intelligent and less qualified taught religion, which required no special academic qualifications even though religion was the basic motive for the Christian schools in the first place. The present need is for celibates less edified by the high academic standards of a world overimpressed with the mind but woefully underimpressed with the place and potential of the will and heart. Educated but unloving man is proving to be really retarded.

When the reign of academe and diploma worship is re-evaluated there is a possibility that the reign of love may begin. The diploma is currently the passport to self-aggrandizement, granted for faithful worship of material progress. Heart must be put into education; man must aspire to be as good as he is smart. Those who learn are smart, but those who love are good. Celibates lost the respect of the world and their own self-respect when they began to accept the same one-dimensional standards of the academic world that are everywhere now coming under fire. Nothing will so restore their position in the world, or their belief in themselves, as the development of their personal power to love and its dedication to the service of the people of God.

The words celibate and loving are contradictory for many, simply because they do not separate the word love from a sexual connotation unrelated to a personal relationship between men and women, priests and nuns. The word love, to celibates, carries a morbid fear of scandal, a cultural heritage from historic mistakes having nothing to do with loving but much to do with pride, arrogance and exploitation. Fearful people, so much more capable of shame for sin than of sorrow, do not grasp the importance of personal love or the awful scandal of personal unloving. Their actions are inspired more by the weakness of sinners than the strength of saints. Honest errors in chastity are surely less of a scandal than power struggles between religious orders, or the ambitions of inflated churchmen daring to stand, without trembling, in the place of God for others. The progress of the people of God requires full-hearted collaboration of loving men and women whose harmonious relationships are irrefutable witness to the virtue which makes chaste and mutually inspiring love between them possible. Such love reveals the exaggeration of genital sexual fulfilment, an emphasis which is so detrimental to real love.

The loving union of Joseph and Mary exemplifies the power of love to transcend sex. Love, not sex, was the basis of their deepest understanding. It is this power to love that the accommodating theologians reject when they cast doubt on the traditional marriage relationship of Joseph and Mary. The sexually dominated, whether positively or negatively, miss the deep meaning in the virginal love relationship, which they would dismiss as fictional. But how ridiculous to concede to Mary a symbolic virginity, as meaningless as it would be dishonest! Such symbolism would be totally unworthy of the God of truth. Celibates and theologians who allow sex to deter them from love project their own fear of sex when they doubt the perpetual virginity of the mother of Christ. It defies their own rules, which they use both to excuse their weaknesses and justify their fears. They underestimate both the potential of man and the grace of God when they repudiate the dangers in loving as abnormal and the occasion of love as beyond grace. The world has small reason to believe in a love which celibates discount because they do not have the virtue to practice it. Virginity is always possible when the deepest bond between two people is true love. Virginity, however, like celibacy, is never Christian if it is unloving.

The celibate who refuses to be sex-dominated, either by fear or by passion, finds that his relationships, guided by the good of others, develop depths of friendship hitherto unsuspected. Loving deeply, he finds himself a real man in the very best sense of the word. Such love is not as far above the ordinary man as some would like to make it. Recorded history is a sparse account of the thousands who, like Thomas More, so loved people and a truthful cause that even their vital needs and life itself were transcended. If sanctity and love are harder than that, then people should forget them, for God has surely set a goal beyond human achievement. Artists and scientists so engrossed in their work that sex is forgotten or ignored show clearly the power of the mind and will to manage the strongest emotions.

The irreversible commitment to celibacy enables the loving person to learn much. As he lives through his first experience of a deep personal love, he clearly understands that marriage is not essential to love, but is a special relationship of its own. He grasps that he can love several people uniquely and still well, and that no one of them ever replaces another. He realizes that, when love is genuine, each loved one develops a deep personal respect for the others, and all are brought much closer in the respect they have for their common loved one. The more genuinely loving is the celibate, the greater the likelihood that his love will be cross-cultural, cross-racial and supranational. The purest form of Christian love is within his reach. His talk of brotherhood rings true, and its authority is instinctively sensed by those with whom he works, and to whom he dedicates his life.

If one has no irreversible commitment or is incapable of respecting the one he has, the shock of "falling in love" is likely to carry the day. However, when in the middle of the loving emotional turmoil one has the discipline to be guided by his commitment, at least to the extent of doing nothing contrary to it, time takes care of the emotional impact and eventually provides clear, incontrovertible proof that celibate love is very real, and truly human. Even if reason does not make it clear, experience will prove beyond doubt how well the celibate loves the lovable person whom he encounters in the course of his work. He will more easily and confidently move through the emotional stages of love with each experience, to live and value the loving relationship which so inspires him and those he loves. The responsibility of celibate love is to use the occasions it provides for the personal growth and maturity of anyone involved. Though one must not discount the pressure of the emotional *now*, the tremendous feeling of the uniqueness of the present experience, none of those truly loved ever mean less than they did during the closest association and involvement, when they witnessed the strength and goodwill of a love which kept them from hurt or harm. One does not love his mother less when, or because, he marries, although he must feel so. The deep thought provoked by the feelings of fickleness from involvement in more than one deep personal love relationship, brings a better understanding of love as God's gift and the work of Divine Providence. So great is love's force for good in one's life, and its inherent power to surmount sex, forgo marriage, and survive every human restriction, that true love can only be from God. Such experience of love enables the celibate to see and love the lovable in people to such a degree that he will hardly experience true loneliness, believe that he is ever unprovided for, or be tempted beyond his strength to exploit the emotional and sexual *now* of any relationship. In so far as man can be so, love will make him free and fruitful. That is fulfilment. He will know, as few do, just how many are the wells of love around him to be tapped, from which will spring living love.

The security that man tries so vainly to find in material possessions, and which Christian teaching insists will be found eventually in God alone, is found to the highest degree on earth in true human love. Love makes people comfortable with each other, secure. So many feminists have, with reason, deplored the exploitation of women by a male-dominated world. Yet the woman celibate with the assurance to love and the security of being loved is immune to it, having a poise and impressiveness that is awesome. She inspires people simultaneously to great love and to high virtue. She is the strong woman behind the great man. Great nuns all have this poise and power and give many men the respectful love and inspiration they need. Such women are not tempted to run from every little threat to their virtue, or to seek protection in the morbid fear of sex, but are quite capable of handling sex as it ought to be handled. Their frustrations do not drive them to the momentary satisfactions of sex, but to a good hard look at themselves for the source of the frustration. Their need for sex is amply compensated for by meaningful and honest affection so rewarding since it is manifested because of what they are rather than for what they have, and depends on esteem for them rather than on the desire to use them.

Loving celibacy is the life of community; frustrated celibacy is its death. Happy community is formed by strong, loving people and consists, not in conformity, but in the harmonious collaboration of free people. Harmony exists only where the individuals freely choose to do what is best for others. The loving celibate generates community spirit because he is committed to the community. Suppression of individuals can no more make happy community than suppression of the emotions makes whole people. Community is neither just devotion to a common cause nor a means of personal salvation; it is what Christianity is all about – a loving life shared as extensively as possible, the kind of life for which genuine celibates are eminently suited. World community will hardly be achieved without them because their lives, well lived, are the strongest argument that one's brother or sister really matters a great deal more than one's personal desires. The truest brotherhood is surely practised by those who hear the word of God and keep it. The Word of God is Love.

Before undertaking the celibate life, a candidate must be sure of the same three things which assure a happy marriage. First, that he or she is certainly going to love personally and deeply. Second, that to do so successfully, he or she must have an appreciable emotional security, some adequacy as a person, and a real awareness of manhood or womanhood. Third, that celibate love, like married love, is quite within the competence of a really good person and requires understanding, purpose and discipline.

There can be no place for delusions in the life of the celibate who is going to love well. His love must begin and endure in truth; deceit, conscious or unconscious, is sure evidence of unloving. When the celibate meets someone to whom he relates well, he must know and accept that the relationship can develop only within the terms of his commitment to celibacy. Both people must fully appreciate and respect the differences between romantic and personal love. They must accept that love for them does not, and cannot, lead to marriage. Neither person is then deceived or deceiving, leading or being led to a predominantly emotional, exclusive or possessive love, typified by infatuation and irresponsibility. Celibate love is truly human, personal, romantic and sexually dimensioned but its outstanding characteristic is its climate of security. It requires inspiring personal integrity, it contributes surely to goodness, it develops deeper interest in God and neighbour. Such love is incompatible with neglect of duty or scandal (that is, real scandal given, not pharisaical scandal taken by small, envious, hostile people).

The person qualified for celibacy must be relatively secure. He meets people with a warm, disarming openness because he has the strength to absorb rejection, and the insight to see it as a weakness in the rejector. He does not have to pursue those he loves, wheedle or cajole them into a response, nor is he such an emotional dependent that he cannot accept the flaws he has and which others actually see in him. He can love people who do not return his love. He can accept the reaction of the fearful and envious without seriously doubting his own adequacy. He can appreciate the inability of the inadequate to accept him at face value, and understands their rejection as their projected fear of his rejection, born of unhappy experience in reaching for things beyond them. An outgoing person, sexually integrated, he appreciates the sexual element in every encounter, and survives the misunderstandings inseparable from loving in today's sex-dominated culture. He is not crushed by the suspicions of the insecure and the envious, nor does he allow them to close off his basic interest in others. He is tolerant, understanding of, and sympathetic to, small people who could not help wanting the relationships he has. He easily recognizes that those so quick to presume bad motives and wrong conduct are merely projecting their frustrated desires and resentment. Because of his own insight, he can understand people and accept them for what they are. He does not mistake genuine response for pursuit, genuine interest for seductive availability. His security gives him the solidity to live well with the risks.

Celibate love makes the lives of those loved more meaningful and efficacious; it is never detrimental. Such relationships with single people may inspire them to the celibate life but never expect, compel or directly suggest it. They never interfere with marital opportunities, but, on the contrary, better prepare the single loved ones for the loving life whether in marriage or celibacy, teaching them to love more deeply and maturely. The loving celibate relationship with a married person contributes to better relationships between the spouses themselves and their children, for which those involved are very grateful. A loving relationship between celibates makes both better fitted for the work they do, the community life they live, and creates in them greater esteem for the people they serve. To those who insist that such love requires heroism, it can only be said that loving, after all, is the highest human achievement, and dedication to loving is the profession of the Christian celibate.

Since love in action is essentially the overflow of abundance, the obvious qualities which the loving celibate brings to his work are notable security, sense of personal worth, insight into and understanding of others. Most people treasure such a person. Far from reducing his availability, the celibate's love lets him give more of himself, adds to what he has to offer, and increases the generosity and effectiveness with which he offers it. He is never deluded that he is more important than anyone can be in the affairs of others, which he refuses to dominate. Whatever his limitations, he achieves the goals of a whole, fine person. He is not pressed by his own needs to lay up treasures on earth; he does not need the reassurance of material things. He understands the scandalized world which cannot believe anyone loves without sexual exploitation, and he pities it. He accepts that the greater scandal by far is not to love at all. He fully appreciates that while the world may not believe when it sees such a love, it can never believe *unless* it sees it.

Naturally, such love must not be wishful thinking, but real. It is a very knowing love fully aware of the limitations of sex, either through experience or understanding; it is an outgoing love that refuses to turn in on itself for satisfaction, or for compensation for rejection or disappointment. The more insecure the celibate, the more naively he reaches out for the expressed love of someone to bolster his ego. Impatient and precipitate, his wishful thinking presumes in others the good qualities he wants to see but which, in fact, are not there. He demands from these people an assurance they are incapable of giving. He presumes relationships prematurely and sees depths in shallow people. He dooms himself to proceed from one disappointment to another, to carry scars from all of them, and ultimately to settle for pleasure rather than love in many casual relationships. Such a celibate soon becomes cynical, self-indulgent, resentful and bitter. He loses all hope of being loved well. He is then as poor a risk in marriage as he was in celibacy. He is typical of the vast majority of people aspiring to be loved without loving, completely oblivious to the fact that there can be no echo where there is no sound. He condemns himself to a life of withdrawal; of addiction to things, which cannot reject him; of unhappiness, which cannot escape him.

Celibates incapable of relating well to the opposite sex are incapable of relating well to anyone, certainly to God. They are fear-dominated, insecure victims of rejection, real and imagined. They have too low an opinion of themselves to hope for acceptance by anyone they consider superior, and they are very afraid that almost everyone is superior. They develop the horrible habit of cutting down anyone better than themselves, of destroying those they would like to love. Withdrawn, they are more fugitive than hermit, more prisoner than recluse. Their reaction to others depends almost entirely on their anticipated reception. Only those capable of unilateral dedication and great love can be patient enough to reach them.

The difference between those interested in people and those on the prowl is that the former want to love, the latter to be loved. To look for a special someone to love is to look for trouble and disappointment since sexual compulsion disguises itself so easily as personal interest. The loving celibate sees lovable people all around him, and in some few he finds people in whom he can invest himself as a person without losing his identity, to whom he can express himself without misunderstanding, in whom his interest evokes an interest as genuine as his own. The loving celibate discovers in those with whom he works many qualities inviting his love, and thus is spared the tragedy of ever looking for someone to love. The people to be loved are always there when needed, though not necessarily when wanted. He does not pass them by unnoticed in a frantic search for someone more to his liking. His interested love, bringing out the best in others, meets response anywhere, everywhere, and encourages other loving persons to team with him very effectively for good. That is why he generates community. His experience in patient love develops a tremendous trust in Divine Providence which enables him to calm his inner turmoil and to love within his commitment. He accepts that his relationship with God made possible his celibacy and thus loves deeply within its context. He never expects people to love him within a context they neither understand nor accept, and thus easily dismisses those whose love would erode his celibacy.

The high respect for celibates is earned precisely by those qualities which make possible their commitment for life to a love without complete sexual fulfilment, however deep and personal it may be. When such qualities actually exist the respect is warranted; when they do not the celibate is a fraud. Celibate commitment makes it possible for the celibate to see the person he loves rather than the fringe benefits; it gives him the detachment and the patience to look for people rather than for superficial attributes; it takes the urgency out of relationships and provides the time to know, understand and communicate, the functions so necessary in enduring married love. Celibate love does not go out to look for love but deliberately interests itself in the neighbour, the next one, those around it, in ever enlarging circles until its interest extends to all. The people all around the celibate require the attention he is uniquely free to give, which, in return, evokes responses leading to lasting friendships, mutual respect and love. It is neither Christian nor loving, but deceitful to offer under the guise of friendship, only what is great and wonderful, breathtaking or priceless. It is honest and loving simply to offer what one has, regardless of its value. Real relationships are gifts, not bribes. Only a lover can bear the burden of gratitude, while so many people find it easier to give generously than to receive graciously. Love is the free exchange of gifts, from each as he has to offer, and to each as he is capable of receiving. Friendships do not exist, nor are people known as friends, unless lives are touched with genuinely given and received interest and concern.

The interested and concerned celibate discovers, as he relates to others, how desperately interest and concern are needed in our world. Moving into this need, he is assured of fulfilment as a human being by loving well. The sexual feelings experienced in the beginnings of friendships, and with which he lives so maturely, make him aware of the responsibility to love well, assure him of his masculinity (or her, of her femininity), and afford evidence of normal emotional health. The prostate, Cowper's and Littre's glandular secretions (or their equivalents in the female, Bartholin's, Skene's, etc.) stimulated by the tenderness of love, challenge him to a moral maturity by integrating the normal sexual feelings accompanying genuine love and affection honestly manifested. The emotional calm of tranquil love dominates the sexual emotions of the celibate whose attention is diverted from his genitals by the good of the whole person loved. Experiencing how secondary the sexual emotions remain under the dominance of genuine love, the celibate learns, more quickly than do married people, how very completely sex can be subjected to the over-all direction of love.

The human body is at the command of the person who loves well. Needless to say, those people who lack the discipline to control their weight, the quantity they drink, their indulgence in pleasure or their flight from pain, will not accept that sex is manageable, simply because, in their indulgent experience, it is not. Certainly the celibate who does not masturbate will not abuse the body of one he loves, nor will one who uses money well, wields authority wisely, or does his job thoroughly, operate irresponsibly in the sexual field when loving. Many things demanded of the convinced Christian are more difficult than living without a full sexual life. The emphasis on Christian celibacy should find the greater emphasis on Christian, and the lesser on celibacy. Certainly one who loves his enemies has sufficient goodwill to govern his emotional life, to insure the integrity of his friends. No greater goodwill is required for celibacy.

To put it bluntly, any celibate who believes that he must love, and does so sensibly, with the virtue required of him as a Christian, let alone a Christian celibate, absolutely refuses to exploit anyone in the name of love. He is so very keenly aware of what is good for himself and for the loved one that every association he has will be dominated by what he knows is right. Like any responsible athlete, he keeps himself in condition, and the condition of love is the respected responsibility at all times for the good of the other. All expression of love and affection in his life is gauged by the capacity of the other to receive it. He is free to relate well and express deep love only to those capable of receiving it within the terms of his commitment to God and the people of God.

For those who timidly insist that celibates should love all people but no one person in particular, it must be insisted that no one can love people in general without loving any one in particular. People are not loved as groups but as individuals. Who does not love one does not really love at all. Who loves no one has not learned to love. It simply cannot be a virtue to love a hundred people but a sin to love one. Authentic celibacy requires that one love each human being humanly. The challenge is to see that as a celibate one does not love sexually, but personally, with a love that has a sexual dimension (as all human love must) but involves the whole person, and which can be open to all forms of expression except the genital function of sexual intercourse.

Celibate love is obviously not some vague, indefinite thing but the love of this particular person for that particular person. It can equally be the love of a man for a man, or of a woman for a woman, but it is always personal, individual and human. But, more than anything else, it is always true, deep and enduring. When loving deeply as celibates, two people share an intimacy in which they reach their loving potential not merely in relation to each other but also in relation to their fellow man and to God. Their love is other-oriented, as all love must be; its essential element is the maturing of both lover and loved; its essential effect is always the growth of the loving persons. Its characteristics are deepening understanding, flexible but solid discipline, greater acceptance of self, and personal sharing excluding only the genital function. Through the full acceptance of his humanity in such loving, the celibate avoids being uptight against frustrating sexual deprivation and passes through sexual awareness to a greater personal interest which leaves sex behind.

For the celibate, as for any mature person, to love is not the same as to "fall in love", though the thrilling discovery of mutual interest and understanding is always accompanied by pleasurable, sensual emotions. Celibate love is not a love between sexes but between sexual persons who relate well to each other, and actually feel it.

The genuine interest strikes the spark of goodness in another and explodes it into the delight of personal loving fulfilment. It is not good for man to be alone; love shows man just how good it is to share. Neither marriage nor celibacy in itself, but the loving relationships lived in either state, keep man from being alone.

Though sex is a human need, a far greater one is the free, open exposure of one's inner self to a loving person, one's self-realization and acceptance in the love of another. Some insight makes it clear that if, in the painful course of one's growth towards wholeness as a person, one turns to sexual exploitation for satisfaction, then one forfeits both the relationship to the other person and one's own greatness of heart. The celibate who is loved deeply will find in that rewarding love the courage to face his own shortcomings and deep-felt needs. He will find his insight into human nature expanded and his availability to those who need him – the rejected, the disillusioned, and the many troubled people who look to him for help – actually increased and enhanced.

The loving situation is the occasion, as well as the test, of emotional security. The Christian celibate loves despite all obstacles. (His failure to do so retards his growth in and understanding of love.) He is not deterred by the frightening experiences inevitable in love, the risks to his integrity, the ever present danger of bad judgment, the frightening anxiety and guilt feelings experienced in going against accepted patterns of behaviour, the envy of the resentful or the demands of the unreasonable. Whatever his feelings, the experience of love makes the celibate stronger and more responsible, increases his happiness and fulfilment, while at the same time making him more easily and readily available to others with an understanding and insight he would not otherwise have. Love for one person increases one's love for all, because love by its nature is expansive. The greater knowledge and understanding that loving people have of each other, the more these same qualities mark their relations with others. Love has inseparable emotional overtones but is essentially based on goodwill. It is the Good News of the gospel that while man can live and grow without many things, he cannot do so without love, the ability to give without strings, without depending on an emotional feedback.

The confrontation with a real loving situation tends to do one of three things to the celibate. First, it may frighten him into flight, and therefore prevent his personal growth and maturity. Second, it may cause him to feel that celibacy is contrary to nature, an unbearable burden, personally inhibiting and destructive, and therefore unacceptable. Third, it may present a challenge to love deeply and well, within the framework of a celibacy willingly accepted for the people of God. The celibates of the third group who could see and accept the challenge to love well, often found themselves an embarrassment to the "system" or to frightened superiors. Unfortunately, few of them could accept disapproval and go on courageously to show the power of Christian love; they either caved in or opted out. Finding themselves shunned or condemned for loving, they either withdrew and built a wall around themselves to avoid further hurt, or said "The hell with the system" and left the priesthood or the religious life, as if the only way to love were in marriage. Thus, by default, celibacy was left to the unloving and seemed essentially an unloving way of life, to be rejected.

Because he so fully accepts his humanity before he commits himself to celibacy, the loving celibate is neither surprised nor upset by its demands. He does not expect to undergo some mystical change of life or nature; he does expect to live as a sexual person, loving but not copulating. Sex is in no way bigger than he is; like any other appetite for pleasure, it is limited to the influence and place in his life that is good for him, without his being tantalized beyond control by that which he has chosen not to have. He accepts all the pain, too, that is required by his own good and that of the people and work involved in his dedication. His sex impulses are accepted in the context of responsibility. The emotional impact of sex does not rob him of the judgment to differentiate between sex and the love which is so much more personal, takes so much longer and goes so much deeper. He is not deluded that celibacy requires supermen, since he is sufficiently "with it" to be aware of many ordinary people confronted daily with sexually stimulating situations which they meet quite casually, without shock, surprise or capitulation. He accepts the reasonable crunch of celibacy as he sees around him the indisputable crunch of normal married life. He moves into loving situations with the sure knowledge that his potential is reached by loving. It is axiomatic for him that there can never be anything wrong with loving, nor will valid love ever lure him from his vocation.

CHAPTER FOURTEEN

Celibate Training

There are two current idioms which should apply to celibate training. They are "to do one's own thing" and "to turn on". The glad willingness to do one's own thing should result in the most meaningful life possible, the most loving life, which would really "turn on" others to genuine loving. Unfortunately, in this day of the emotional binge, the word meaningful merely means enjoyable. Christ's death on the cross could hardly be described as enjoyable, although it is the most meaningful event in Christianity. Love is surely the most meaningful human experience, but it is by no means always the most enjoyable. The celibate more than most human beings does his own thing if "his thing" means growing to his fullest stature, being everything that God would have him be, has given him the potential to be. In making his lifelong commitment to Christ, he accepts that he can actually "do all things in Him who strengthens him". This "thing" which he does, then, makes him tremendously loving and therefore gives him the truly divine power to "turn people on", to help people find in loving their highest fulfilment. No one could be more fully human or have a greater mission to man.

To teach mankind to love, celibacy requires the equality of men and women. Love establishes equality because it always speaks as an equal to man or woman. The institutional Church has a fair, if blemished, record as liberator of women. The Church does not act out of the context of history, for she is actually the people of God in their journey through history. But she could have done better, is doing better, and will do better yet. Despite their tremendous contributions as Christians over the ages women were not admitted to the early Councils of the Church, and were only belatedly admitted to Vatican II, in the role of observers. With little sense of incongruity, men have always made the rules for the congregations of women, and generally, without advice or consent, imposed and supervised these rules. Women have seldom, if ever, been encouraged to play the role for which their intelligence, virtue and extraordinary qualifications have suited them. They have been called the weaker sex despite overwhelming evidence in many areas of living of a strength surpassing that of men. Only the superiority of women, in most instances, enabled them to achieve their goals despite oppression. By guile, wile and smile they unzipped the male egos for many good purposes. Women, given their rightful place in the church, speaking as equals though different, will exercise excellent influence just because, culturally, they have been freer to love than have men. Far from impeding progress in holiness, true loving relationships make the lives of all people really meaningful, creative and productive. Loving celibate women have always been a source of strength, inspiration and support for celibate men, and vice versa. It is through their very love that lack of sexual function has been acceptable, and even inspiring.

Celibate training should be positive conditioning to live the best way, rather than the "safest" way. The best, and in fact the only way, is the loving way, a risky but good and necessary way. It remains a mystery just how celibates, so familiar with the fate of the man in the gospel who buried his talent to avoid losing it, could ever canonize the "safe" way. Only now, in the face of near collapse of celibate life, are celibates encouraged to develop their own minds, strengths, personal judgments and consciences, urged to reject unreasonable demands and the imposed discipline so destructive of personal integrity. Suddenly it seems reasonable that celibates be equal to the risks of being fully human. Being human was previously synonymous with being weak, despite the fact that God made people human. Only when celibates are whole human beings, thinking, loving people, will authentic Christian celibacy flourish again in service to the people of God. Love, rather than sexual suppression, will be the insurance against sin. Truly loving celibates illustrate, as no others can, the difference between love and sex.

The authentic celibate teaches, by word and example, that mature people are capable of loving relationships. Sexual segregation of celibates sets unacceptable limits to virtue, and accepts the immaturity of the dedicated as normal. Holiness is certainly beyond people who cannot be chaste in the normal course of human relationships, whose chastity depends on cloister rather than virtue. Celibate men often manifest distinct discomfort in the presence of women, a visible reluctance to be alone with them for any reason, however good. Such situations were habitually presented to them as all but insuperable obstacles to virtue. Many women rightly resent this implication of their lack of virtue. However, those women with greater security and insight, to say nothing of some real virtue, correctly read into such discomfort serious doubts by the celibate of his own virtue, and some real sex hang-ups. Such reaction to them plainly attributed to women a predatory attitude impossible to cope with, and so made pastoral neglect of women seem a virtue. The situation is paralleled in the lives of celibate women who make a virtue of being hostile to men, seeking an ersatz safety in that hostility. Any such celibates who do not develop a thoroughly unchristian meanness are nearly unnerved by the presence of the opposite sex; the more attractive the person the more unnerved the celibate, and the more obviously shallow the virtue. Many of them become fair game for the sophisticated iconoclast who rightly resents such presumed virtue, so patently unequal to the tests of normal life. This kind of "holiness" is irrelevant in a sexually integrated, permissive society, which desperately needs to see some genuine virtue. Teaching love is the job for people whose interest in others transcends sexual fulfilment. Adequately instructed in sexual matters, foreseeing loving futures fertile in friendships as rewarding as the happiest of marriages, such celibates can prepare young people for living lovingly in marriage or celibacy.

Acceptance of grace and the supernatural are always presumed in discussing celibacy; they should certainly be seen as necessary to live it. True celibacy requires a thorough understanding of sex. Personal sexual experience is not necessary for this but an efficiently functioning imagination is mandatory. Like the emotions, to which it is nearly as closely related as it is to the mind, the imagination can be used well, suppressed, or exploited. Nothing can excuse ignoring it. The creative realist who uses it well will find that it quite adequately replaces most learning experience for him. Through the well used imagination, happy and effective celibates experience the sexual aspects of their humanity. Such imagination enables celibate love to pass from the talking stage into reality by making plain the risks in loving, for which the virtuous person is prepared.

The celibate who lives his sexual life vicariously, by exploiting his imagination, makes genuine celibacy impossible and his own life very unhappy. He identifies love with lust and to secure himself, often develops a tyrannical, harsh meanness, totally unworthy of the Christian vocation and verging on emotional illness. A highly esteemed and well used imagination is probably one of the best assurances of emotional and mental health, and the emotionally healthy person can fully accept and live celibacy; the unhealthy cannot. Even the most genuine effort to love on the part of the emotionally crippled brings grief, tension, unhappiness and frustration which usually lead either to the lonely bitterness of isolation or to the abandonment of vocation. Suppression of the imagination, as a supposed source of temptation, assures the unhappiness of celibates, for whom imaginative creativity must replace the loving procreativity of parenthood. Those who suppress the imagination rob themselves of the means to recognize the substitutes for sex and love, things as spiritually detrimental as the abuse of sex itself. They usually fail completely to understand sex, and often sublimate their sexual dimension into devotion to the system, from which they seek and receive authority which casts them in roles signifying, to themselves, God's approval. They find their outlets in money, travel, recreation and many other fringe benefits that replace their personal growth through love.

Celibate love has been hedged about with endless legalities born of morbid fears and very definite negations which make the Good News hardly worth mentioning. Sex is the material of celibacy, so the celibate must be thoroughly conversant with it, rather than morbidly intrigued by it. Only that celibate can remain celibate today who can live with the sexual emotions. Many of those disenchanted with celibate life suddenly discovered their sexual emotions, and, in the present fetish for involvement, found themselves completely unprepared to cope. The very real emotional experiences, both pleasant and painful, which are the normal preliminaries to actual loving utterly confused them. They simply did not get the message from their emotions to look the situation in the face and assess that situation for what it really was. The emotional impact of love is no different in its purpose from any other emotional impact – anger, jealousy, depression, resentment or elation. When he first relates to a lovable and appealing member of the opposite sex the celibate must expect to feel like a person in love – distracted, excited, his thoughts continually moving to the loved one. However, none of these feelings need rob him of the judgment to know that loving is far more than emotional impact, which is only the barest beginning. With discipline he has the strength to move through feeling "in love" to actual loving. To retreat from loving overtures as temptations, or occasions of sin, is to prevent the maturing growth and confirmation of celibacy itself. It is simply to refuse to develop the power to love required by celibate living, and to condemn oneself to an ineffectual ministry.

Morbid fear of sex makes ignorance seem a virtue. "What they don't know won't hurt them" is the poorest excuse for lack of sex instruction in celibate training. We are now experiencing how wrong that attitude is. Ignorance of sex permits it to assume proportions far beyond reality, and to promise rewards far beyond its capacity to bring. That ignorance makes celibacy seem cruel, and marriage a sure promise of personal fulfilment. Surely the fact that God created it should have made sex worthy of celibate study and understanding; yet, culturally as well as religiously, God and sex have been all but mutually exclusive. It is God's plan for sex that makes sexual exploitation, in or out of marriage, wrong, and the use of sex in marriage a worthy way of expressing the deepest human love. Knowledge of sex, combined with virtue, enable the celibate to experience sexual maturation with awareness and understanding. He can then accept that full experience of sexual feelings without compulsion to the sexual function is as normal as the experience of feelings of deep anger without exploding in a rage. Ignorance of the real limitations of sex encourages in celibates, as it does in all persons, a morbid fascination with sex, an exaggeration both of its urgency and its pleasure. It makes the risk in the Christian's solemn obligation to love seem too great, requiring celibate love to be angelic or at least superhuman, sexless rather than merely without genital function.

Fear of the opposite sex backed some celibates into homosexuality; others naively mistook their predilection for members of their own sex for "community". Still others capitulated to the exaggerated importance of sex and judged themselves incapable of celibacy. For almost all, the danger of sexual sin was seen as far greater than the tragedy of not loving at all. The power of sex to enslave was conceded, almost without argument, to be greater than the power of love to liberate. Had celibates really understood it well, sex could never have become for them more a matter of shame than of proud acceptance. Ignorance of sex severely handicapped the celibate in advising and counselling his people in sexual matters. Uninformed and fearful himself, he was in no position to explain to the people how sex was to be used well for the great good of man, without himself feeling it indispensable. Quite probably the generally poor management of sex by so many can be attributed largely to encouraged ignorance of it, or worse, its condemnation by silence, born of ignorance on the part of fearful instructors.

The celibate's understanding of sexual maturation, which enables him to live at cruising speed with his sexual emotions and to exercise the proper conduct in sexual situations, also qualifies him to help married people ensure that love will be the dominant force in their sexual lives. He is able to counsel them to move through the shoals of sex to loving personal realationships. Proper instruction removes the delusion of sexual feelings as contraindications to the celibate life. Learning to live with one's sexual emotions brings much subconscious tension to the surface, where it can be managed. Unbearable tension is reduced to manageable proportions by detailed, graphic sex information which minimizes its mysteries and eliminates morbid curiosity. Adequate sex instruction does not free from the pressure of sex but from the devastating *fear* of sex.

Proper sex instruction solves the conflict so many celibates experience in innocent loving relationships, when the sexual glands, responding as they do to feelings of tenderness, create the anxiety leading to responsible action. The sexual emotions are blind faculties which react automatically, without discernment, to the stimulus of loving, unless inhibited. Although differing in degree and intensity from a full genital sexual reaction, there is a minimal sexual response to any loving situation which proper understanding enables the celibate to accept without qualm or undue concern. It is precisely through this understanding that he uses the series of inhibiting mechanisms available to his mind and will in thoughtful loving. Ignorance, on the contrary, creates dismay and apprehension which lead him to confuse feelings for motives, anxiety for guilt, mechanical effects for deliberate acts. A moderate genital excitation is a healthy fact of emotional life, without moral overtones, and is the greatest help to the celibate in directing his loving to the person loved rather than to himself. As celibates understand and accept these happenings, they will gradually emerge from fear of sex, and fully accept their humanity and wholeness as people.

Despite the admitted obligation to love, some question the possibility of real love in interpersonal, intersexual relationships without the use of the genital sex function. The difficulty comes from the impossibility of drawing clear, comfortable lines between right and wrong in the honest effort to love. The "be sure you are right" moral theology replaced the more Christian "be sure you love" theology. The determination to love despite unresolved problems produced the now famous "Third Way" as an accommodation between celibacy and marriage. While the Third Way is variously defined, it generally means in fact the best of both worlds in compensation for the "sacrifice" of home and family. Too many, under the real or imagined sexual exigency, threw themselves into this way of life without first defining its limits or understanding its implications. Many who thus accepted genital sex as an inseparable part of loving man-woman relationships left the priesthood or religious life for an underground church where they could have their cake and eat it too. To propose a full sexual life without marriage is to endorse "free love", more correctly called free sex, and is to take privileges without obligations. It is dishonest, cheating, and exploitation worthy neither of God nor of love. For others, the Third Way meant the loving relationship with the sexual emotions neither exploited nor suppressed but lived with, maturely and responsibly – really the Christian Way. To do this, however, many wrongly left communities where suspicions reigned and formal relationships were required that thinly disguised complete lack of interest. They had not the courage to love despite the censure of the insecure and envious. The Christian Way of loving is in fact the First Way, Christ's Way, the way in which celibates must be trained to love – humanly, honestly, well and personally.

The Christian celibate accepts without question that the sexual function is restricted to husbands and wives, fathers and mothers, who make a permanent commitment of full, personal and exclusive availability incompatible with celibate life. The honest celibate could not possibly believe that he truly loves while using contraceptives in a full sexual relationship. The Christian, expressing love through the genitals, does not have to take precautions against the very effects of his love. Sex can never, even momentarily, play the dominant role between friends, however close, who intend to remain unmarried. The genital sex function used out of marriage deprives any relationship of the security and respect essential to true love.

The loving relationship of Joseph and Mary should be the model of all celibate relationships. The fact of the marriage of Joseph and Mary would seem to rule this out, though in reality it is the erroneous conviction of the indispensability of sexual intercourse, rather than the fact of their marriage, that casts doubt on the virginal chastity of Joseph and Mary. The concept that love can make sexual intercourse superfluous to any relationship seems incredible to many people. It was undoubtedly this mentality which caused Joseph to be depicted for centuries as an old man. However, had he really been an old man he could hardly have supported Jesus and Mary by his labours, nor could he have made the arduous journey into Egypt, and have afforded Mary the protection she undoubtedly needed along the way.

It also must be considered whether Joseph actually slept with Mary. The thought that they slept in tender. loving proximity should offend no one for surely this represented their actual relationship. Geography does not purify the heart, nor does distance constitute virtue. The lust which ends up in bed does not begin there. The deep love that makes a man respect a woman enables him to sleep with her without sexual intercourse if such a thing is necessary or desirable for any reason. Christ made it plain that lust, not sex, is sinful; that chastity is not a matter of segregation or walls but of loving well. If, as many of the moral theologians have insisted, it is an occasion of sin for a man and a woman to be alone, then Mary and Joseph lived in one long occasion of sin, and her virginity has to be, at best, in doubt. But, if the love of God and dedication to His purposes make one virtuous and loving, if chastity is the virtue of loving deeply and well, if God really was the centre of the lives of both Joseph and Mary long before they came together, then deep love was their form of communication and sex had nothing to add to their closeness and sharing. Joseph and Mary have relevance for us because they differ from us only in the degree of their love for God and for each other. Not only did the love of Joseph and Mary make the thought of seeking each other apart from God's plan for both of them unthinkable, but it made being together tremendously meaningful. Theirs was the most personal of relationships.

The eager mutual support of the love of Joseph and Mary made the anguish of their responsibility for Christ bearable. Their deep union as loving people made sexual intercourse superfluous, as does the union of any couple mutually intent on something more important than their own personal needs. Genital sex, like words, has a very limited power to express love. Mary and Joseph, being human, had their sexual feelings, but those feelings could not distract them from what held them so firmly, their life with Christ in God. It was not that they were superhuman, devoid of sexual feelings or divinely anaesthetized, as many oblivious of the spellbinding power of love would believe. It was just that their sexuality was so integrated into their humanity that the sexual function itself was powerless to add anything more to their love. It was as simple as that. The same sexual integration can be experienced by anyone willing to love enough. Such love is well within the human potential, and many do achieve it. It is well within the potential of anyone who dedicates himself for life to the people of God, a God in whose power he deeply believes and through whose power he so deeply loves. Celibates in training must have it impressed on them that, while many people do not and will not develop their power to love, no one can expect to be effectively celibate who does not do so.

It is quite ridiculous to consider the female less sexual than the male. Culturally, lust has been expected and even admired in the male while widely despised or denied in the female. The female celibate is not exempt from the feelings of the ordinary woman, or her sexual needs. Her celibacy is the equally willing forfeit of a sexual fulfilment she very much desires in order to achieve the loving life so vital to herself and others. She does not opt for celibacy despite her sexual needs, but in full awareness and acceptance of them. The celibate woman, keenly aware of her desire for sexual union with many of the good men with whom she works, acquires the virtue to love deeply without the genital sex function. Some do mistake for celibacy the withdrawal into unrealistic sterility to avoid sexual involvement. Many of these later discover their humanity and sexuality under the pressure of personal crises. They one day find themselves suddenly and desperately aware of the need they have so long misunderstood and suppressed. Their only protection then is the lack of opportunity – which for too long has been the main line of defence for religious whose virtue is not equal to the test.

Celibate love is the will to give the good of the loved priority without restriction over one's own sexual need and urge. To deny the sexual dimension and urge in celibate love is to deny the humanity of celibates. St. Paul made it abundantly clear that only grace and faith made it possible for him to contend with his sexual urge and to so love people as to be celibate for life in their service. The ability to live with the full blast of the sexual emotions is required for virtuous living in the world of people, half of whom are of the opposite sex, and 80 percent of whom are lonely. The complete integration of sex and its emotions enables the celibate to be as loving as a husband or wife, with an interest in others which is solicitous rather than seductive, loving rather than amorous, sexual rather than sexy, intimate rather than exclusive.

CHAPTER FIFTEEN

Celibate Hang-ups

The celibate must not dismiss sex as less than it really is, or expect love somehow to obliterate sexual awareness and its problems. Such a mistake makes it impossible for him to negotiate the dangerous channels of emotional involvement to the deeper personal relationship. Pleasurable sex emotions (feelings) make it difficult for any person in a sexual situation to give the personal relationship priority over the sexual. But anyone who accepts the full power of sex, and measures it against the power to love can do it. The mature awareness of the sexual element in every relationship enables the celibate to accept sex without being overwhelmed by it. He does not grasp at sex as an antidote for loneliness, inadequacy or insecurity. A celibate must experience and understand the inescapable pleasure of sex and accept it without fear or guilt. He must not equate pleasure with sin, or accumulated pleasure with happiness.

Sexual frustration, so easily and falsely attributed to celibacy by those who erroneously assume that sexual fulfilment is automatic in marriage, is common to both states. It is typical of the self-indulgent who expect so much more of sex than it can provide, while rare in those who use sex well, or, fully accepting it, choose not to use it at all. Both celibate and married persons find endless frustration in a sexuality which does not lead to loving relationships. The sexually frustrated celibate sees sex as a forbidden outlet for the personal tensions and frustrations in his life. He simply cannot cope with sex, and is as unable to live with it as without it. The sexual frustration of marriage consists largely in the inability to grow in loving through the sexual function, which too easily sidetracks people into self-indulgence.

Discipline is essential to celibate loving. Even externally imposed discipline, however inadequate, is better than none at all. Imposed discipline is so much easier than personal discipline. The rebels against imposed discipline complain that it shows a lack of confidence in mature people. However, they soon discover, to their sorrow, that throwing off the yoke does not dispense with the need for harness. Even tyranny is a relief from the chaos of undiscipline. The modern celibate, unprotected by monastic walls and rigid segregation of the sexes, is defenceless without virtue, his power over self. Any meaningful interpersonal relationship demands it. The priest-worker movement foundered on the point of personal discipline. The good-guy priest without discipline is quickly addicted to his own image and sooner, oftener than later, cops out of a career of selflessness, Christlikeness.

The man who is too sexual to love as a celibate will be too undisciplined to love faithfully in marriage. The celibate who ignores the gravitational pull of sex is as stupid as the married man who thinks he loves because he copulates. The former will remain celibate about as long as the latter remains faithfully married. The celibate who loves with full sexual awareness can be at home in sexual situations only because he is disciplined. It is for the undisciplined that the warnings against sexual situations are so valid. Even honest attempts at loving by the undisciplined produce such tensions and misunderstandings that they are either futile or disastrous. Discipline places sex into the over-all plan of one's life, and respects that plan.

Discipline, real virtue – that is, the power to do what ought to be done (a matter of conviction, not merely of feelings) – restricts the expression of physical affection to the actual rather than the anticipated relationship. Such restriction affords friendship the time it takes to grow into understanding love. Honest affection expresses truth not merely one's feelings, and is given and received as needed regardless of the feelings. It is neither capricious nor self-indulgent. It does not play games nor conflict with any other obligation or commitment; it refuses to put the loved one to a test which will not be met successfully. Honest celibate affection is that of people loving, not of people courting. The emotional charge in honest affection is safely cushioned in the discipline of personal fulfilment rather than of self-denial, that is, in the desire to reach one's potential. Honest affection is always within the power of those dedicated to the interest of many, rather than of one exclusively. The affection of those in love, and courting, is legitimately oriented to ultimate sexual intercourse in a loving married life; celibate affection is oriented to the loving life without genital function. The discipline in either case is not greater than needed later in married life, and may be less, for it is often easier to forgo sex entirely than to restrict it to one person, or to such times as it has real meaning for both people in the marriage.

Normal expressions of physical affection are sure to be misused and misunderstood by celibates unless they first relate well to those they love in almost every other way. True celibate affection is never premature nor are the emotions accompanying it the result of affection's stimulus, but of genuine love. The loving emotions of celibate love are evoked by the goodness of the one loved, gradually discovered through discerning interest over a long period of close association. Even people of great intelligence and integrity are too easily convinced, under the stimulus of prematurely manifested affection, that they have a real loving relationship. Basic good sense would preclude the possibility of so deep a relationship on such short association. It is difficult to know oneself after a lifetime of awareness, yet many would rashly assume, under the impact of proximity and affection, that they know others well in almost no time at all. The prevailing force of premature, physical affection is emotional, exploitative, well described as "much wanting more". Discipline makes acceptable whatever pleasure or privation love indicates as best. Emotional love is impatient; it chafes under the pressure of the emotional *now*. Personal love is patient; it has a lifetime to grow. Genuine affection causes the relationship to flourish; it increases both parties' availability and usefulness to others. Exploitative affection exhausts it. Real love, which is never lost, can afford to wait because in its constant growth it holds great promise of happiness. Dishonest, superficial affection cannot wait but is quickly sought in other places when not immediately available here and now. The foolproof sign of maturity is the ability to give and receive honest, lust-free affection.

The striking quality of celibate love is the availability to others which precludes exclusivity. Those who love the celibate have to be big people, able to live with feelings of jealousy and possessiveness without being jealous or possessive. The celibate himself, however, must not be compelled by his image to become public domain without any private life of his own. Nothing puts him more uptight than living the *image*. No one without a personal life is really a person. Personal growth requires privacy, solitude and individual communication. The real person respects his own limitations, and takes the time to develop his potential through prayer, solitude, and the refreshment of soul and body found in private conversation and understanding.

Genuine celibacy is never imposed. It is an act of love, and of its very nature free. Although nearly every priest in the Latin Rite is required to make the personal decision for celibacy, it is not surprising that those who subsequently find the crunch of celibacy greater than expected, or something for which they are inadequately prepared, feel strongly that celibacy was imposed on them because of their desire to become priests. It is difficult to distinguish the revolt against celibacy from revolt against the authority which imposed celibacy as a condition for the priesthood. However, the rationale for calling such celibacy imposed is very thin. Those who considered the priesthood were willing to be celibate. However negative their attitude to a calling requiring positive love, they still willed consent. General abuse of authority created the backlash against it and many celibates used that backlash as a way out of their celibate commitments. Some did so rightfully, because their commitment lacked validity in the first place. They did not really understand or mean what they said. Some do not develop the character to love enough for a lasting commitment.

Optional celibacy cannot mean, as many would have it, two ever open alternatives, which is actually a decision never made. Such people want the best of two different worlds, to have their cake and eat it too. This is the pseudo-celibacy of those who, while professing celibacy, have all the sexual privileges of marriage in the name of love, which they define to suit themselves. When "optional" means a way out of an impossible situation, one can be sure that any situation can look impossible to the small-minded and the selfish, who have no stomach for the very real obligations assumed in loving truly. There can be no built-in escape from the obligations of love, celibate or married. No escape is wanted from the real freedom and security which true love provides. To accept the fact that men quite often find their love situations impossible is one thing, to honour them for doing so is another. The impossibility comes from self, rather than the loving situation. Love in any relationship eludes few celibates or married people willing to work hard enough at it. Certainly that celibacy is meaningless which requires a different type of man or woman from those entering marriage. The celibate must feel the same attraction for the opposite sex, the same sexual inclinations, desires and needs, the same need to love and be loved. He must be capable of the same lifetime commitments, and relationships which are loving, forgoing only the right to be mother or father, husband or wife, or to withhold himself from those who need him. He forfeits only a single way of expressing love, that is, by the genital sex function with its associated privileges and responsibilities. He certainly cannot refuse to love, which is to withdraw from Christian living.

Thus optional celibacy has to be a delusion. The celibate *always* retains his personal and legal freedom to marry. The "optional" celibate has only a bachelor's reason for his celibacy and that is not enough. Although I personally question even Rome's power to dispense anyone from a valid vow made to God to remain forever unmarried out of love for God's people, today there is easy opportunity for the celibate to obtain merciful declaration of freedom to marry in those cases where he seeks it, even dishonestly. (And I don't suppose that such dishonesty is any worse than other forms of deceit everywhere so acceptable.) Love needs and seeks no options, and the celibate, unlike the bachelor, has already opted for his way to manifest his love. To retain an option is to make no choice. Celibacy does not actually deprive the celibate of his freedom to marry, any more than marriage deprives one of his freedom to remarry while his spouse is alive. Love, the essence of freedom, does this. Only trial marriage can follow trial celibacy, which is what optional celibacy really is.

I do believe that when a married man is so recognizably good that the people of God opt to have him ordained a priest, and he himself so desires, provision should be made to ordain him, as it sometimes is. But this is indeed a far cry from optional celibacy. The vast majority of those who advocate the latter are priests who have opted out, publicly or privately, who want to keep their public, priestly image when they have broken their solemn promise, freely made for life as lovingly as they were capable of doing, just because that life has proved more difficult than they had envisioned, and/or they have unexpectedly found someone without whom they feel they cannot live meaningfully. It is impossible for anyone to break a promise without feeling inferior or unfaithful. But those who do not love enough to keep their word (which they can but will not keep) are inferior, as anyone must be who through his own fault remains less than he could be.

Many celibates find in the establishment, the structural Church, an ideal outlet for the dutiful energy and dedication which they would have invested in the formation of a family. Being competent and provident, as most dedicated people are, they aspire to and often attain positions of authority and prominence. They then perpetuate themselves in those positions, not in their own children but by rewarding the loyalty of their spiritual sons and daughters. This is called the "system", whereby those faithful and loyal go up, while those who doubt, question or rebel are punished as disloyal to God, from whom all authority comes. (This system is by no means restricted to the Church.

It prevails on all fronts of the human condition, the business and social order, from labour unions through the halls of academe. The politics of human life, however sad, are inseparable from being human.) Since abused authority and obedience are both approval-oriented, the defiant and revolutionary express their opposition by seeking disapproval. They find in celibacy a natural vehicle for revolution against authority and the system which perpetuates so many abuses.

Most celibates are especially attracted, by their home environments, to an approval-oriented society. In the past generation the prevalent puitanical morality developed such a suspicion of affection that many good parents dutifully omitted necessary manifestations of physical affection for their children. The closest permissible thing to affection, in many good Christian homes, became the approval of parents, and this was eagerly sought by the children. Many children of such homes then entered celibate life, where the only acceptable form of affection was the approval of superiors. This approval was avidly sought by the eagerly loyal, who willingly identified their superiors with God and His approval. Great conflicts befell people who loved the truth but desperately needed approval. They wanted to know, love and serve the truth, but rather naively expected to be approved for doing so by superiors who too often, in typical human weakness, took the truth for what they personally (honestly or dishonestly) wanted it to be. Those whose need for approval was greater than their love for truth caved in and became loyal subjects, praised by superiors for doing what they were told, whether they should have done so or not. Rewarded by the system for continued immaturity and weakness, they in their turn found themselves in positions of authority from which they perpetuated the system. As superiors they were victims, as well as perpetrators, of the "I represent God for you" mentality. They accepted themselves as stand-ins for God, as if God were not quite capable of taking care of Himself, as if the truth, justice, mercy and charity were not better indications of His presence and power than authority arbitrarily abused in His name.

Since personal loyalty to superiors, right or wrong, was equated with loyalty to God and truth, the whole system then wrongfully defended inadequate and even culpable superiors lest the concept of authority be challenged. Things which could not be overlooked, even out of personal loyalty, were made acceptable by the canonization of "community loyalty", even though that sometimes involved treason to God. The end result now is general contempt for authority itself and all that is closely tied to it. However, tyranny is generally overthrown by tyranny, and now the lives of even Christian revolutionaries are seldom marked by greater love and truth than the lives of those they so roundly condemn. People do not prove their love for the poor by insulting the rich, their solidarity with the black by scorning the white, their understanding and tolerance of minorities by abusing the majorities. So intent are the rebels on doing their own thing that they fail to see that authority was abused precisely by doing *its* own thing.

It is eminently right to reject abused authority and unloving celibacy, but in no way is loving celibacy or rightful authority to be rejected. The proper training of celibates must present clear evidence that authority rightly exercised and genuine loving celibacy inspire respect and provide security. Real authority and true love are facts of life that remain through every day of reckoning. They are the constants in Christian life. It takes a strong man to exercise authority responsibly; it takes a strong man to love well, in celibacy or in marriage. The answer is not revolt, but virtue and discipline, the qualities of the strong and the good.

The exodus from religious life and the priesthood has forced the pace of renewal. From the ashes of the establishment are rising the dedicated Christians and celibates who refuse to pass wrongs for rights, weaknesses for strength. Modern religious are detaching themselves from the structures which would take them to their destruction, to strike out for themselves as restive children must when unduly supervised by fearful and overanxious parents. The climate of freedom necessary for the development of love is now being established, though many, unfortunately, confuse it with licence or find it intolerable, too dangerous and frightening.

The ground shock of Vatican II, unnerving religious and lay Catholics alike, is causing not so much the crumbling of reality as the passing of the "glorious" priest-religious-celibate image. Celibate life promises as much and certainly no less than before. There are not fewer genuine vocations, just fewer little people seeking to become ten feet tall in a career which never really promised instant gianthood. The man who was the priest never quite fitted the heroic mold in which he was cast by the ideals of the priesthood. At one time the priesthood itself seemed a real thing. It actually exists only in the people who are priests. The priest is being examined today and being found no greater than life size, a man like other men, with troubles and problems which are the stuff of life. Those who feel disillusioned by this truth seek a new delusion, a bigger role or vocation – the psychologist, counselor or social worker; the man the people need; the academic degrees which people respect regardless of the personal competence of their holders. People want to appear bigger than they really are. They cannot stand exposure or the disappointment when the order they belong to or the office they hold does not add lustre to their names or persons. Only those who live simple, loving lives escape delusions and give glory to God and to man by being people at their best. What is needed badly today is not *good priests* but good people who are priests and religious.

The priestly *image* dispensed celibates from many of humanity's problems; to it they sacrificed the distinction of being very human Christians who loved unusually well. Nothing less than perfection was the tolerable goal for the celibate lifted high by the ideal of this image. Every aspect of living was tailored to the pursuit of a strange holiness by which men left their humanity behind and aspired to the state of near angels. Superhuman stature was accepted as a grace of state. Those who held steadfast to this image became beady-eyed zealots in hot pursuit of the Holy Grail of the impossible. The image drove would-be saints to relentless demands on themselves in atonement for the laziness of their associates. By ulcerative abstemiousness they made amends for their overeating, overdrinking fellows; by withdrawal from everyone they atoned for the infidelities of others. They could not live with themselves if they had any personal preferences or desires. The image they projected did not so much please God as enable them to live securely with themselves. Too proud for adultery, too frightened to drink, too straightlaced for fun, they were much too "holy" to love. The priests unwilling or unable to pursue this image escaped into isolation because they had little sense of their own worth, and almost nothing to say. They built walls against a scrutiny they could not meet. Silence spared them the confrontation with truth that community provides. Devotion to minutiae, legalism and formality let them meet the criteria for priestly functionaries, and spared them putting their ghastly on the line by loving. But most settled for less, some almost for nothing. When the myth of perfection exploded, those unprepared for the cost of love decided to live as they saw fit, at least sexually, if not lovingly.

The image made people feel obliged to apologize when using any vulgarity before the priest, however innocuous, common or acceptable. The priest chafing under this obnoxious image, who used earthy language in protest, even though it was no more than common slang, was considered a scandal. Although a full-grown man, he was expected to be locked safely in the rectory by 11 p.m. As was hypocritically expected of Jesus Christ before him, he, too, was to associate only with those above reproach. When he stood daily before the altar to protest, as priests had done for centuries, that he had sinned, not slightly but exceedingly, not only in thought, which might have been overlooked as understandable and acceptable, but also in word and deed, no one in the church believed him – least of all himself. The further exaggeration meant little as he then went on to say that he was not deceived or seduced but had done it all through his own fault, yes, through his most grievous fault. Had the people really believed him they would have run him out of town, or his fellow priests would have felt compelled at least to report him to the chancery!

Celibate training was almost entirely negative. Zeal for purity made it loveless; to assure its detachment, friendlessness was made a virtue. Thoughts about sex, however positive, were equated with sexy thoughts and considered occasions of sin. The normal pleasure of feeling sexual was rejected as a part of the human condition beneath the priestly life. Cold, arbitrary, disinterested authority usurped the role of loving Father revealed to man by Christ. Few demanded, or even expected, that authority wielded in the name of God should be handled in a way worthy of God. To love was to betray God. Not only were women considered a threat to men and vice versa, but there was a morbid fear of homosexuality underlying many of the rules governing community life. All companionship was suspect. The particular friendships in the life of Christ, if alluded to at all, were dismissed by His Divinity, His difference, which for many made Him irrelevant.

The automatic grace of the sacraments was stressed to the virtual denial of the actual graces available through Christian living. Holiness became a game in which small people, incapable of the greatness to love, sought recognition and attention through false mysticism, extraordinary austerities and penances. Sterile regulations replaced the Spirit; sin came to represent not the rejection of God by man but the quite incongruous rejection of man by God. Such dread consequences of this rejection were presented that good men became far too fearful to love. So gradual was the process of false spirituality that few realized until too late that religious life had become the very antithesis of early Christianity epitomized in the words, "By this shall all men know that you are my disciples, that you love one another." Love was banned and isolation, the escape hatch for the inadequate and insecure, was wrongly identified with the very solitude in which one ponders loving.

So efficient was this system of isolation in community living that few who left celibate life had a single friend to whom they could turn, well in advance of their exodus, for a baring of soul and critical examination of the factors involved in leaving. Few had enough confidence in their associates to expose their emotional conflicts and spiritual turmoil, just because any friendship deeper than casual detachment was suspect. The privacy required for personal counseling was considered unhealthy intimacy rather than opportunity for healthy understanding. Celibates could then in no way be prepared for the deep intimacy of one who touches not merely the body of the confidant but the far deeper and more moving intimacy of the emotions, the understanding, the spiritual life, and the very soul.

"Custody of the eyes", a repudiation of one of the God-given senses through which all knowledge necessarily comes, and which everyone needs to use as well as possible, became a virtue. The imagination which goes wild when blinkers are put over the eyes was then suppressed, in the name of God, as a source of temptation. Both these things took place without the slightest realization that the process had to lead to a deadly lack of interest in people and things, to ill manners and discourtesy. What custody of the eyes began, monastic silence finished – the production of tense, lonely, alienated people for whom silence did not so much eliminate sin as conceal it. Under the guise of godliness religious became complacent islands of self-interest, dedicated only to their personal salvation. Not only were the sick and oppressed often neglected because of the silence, but genuine charity and healthy relationships were sacrificed to conformity.

Disclipline for celibates meant one thing, flight. There was no question of developing the virtue required to love. Mortification, too, had a nearly totally negative connotation – deny oneself pleasure, kill one's desires, rather than use pleasure properly and direct it well. One was praised for living in the deep freeze of unfeeling. By deadening the feelings, so necessary in loving situations, one disqualified oneself for loving, the very stuff of Christian living. Celibate discipline negatively placed great reliance on the "panic button", which disregarded the sure Providence of God. God would just not save one from "rash" exposure to the unwarranted danger supposed to exist in perfectly normal association of the sexes, a duty danger in the priesthood. The outstretching of hands in prayer to God, without the conviction of sure help in the honest effort to love, became a theatrical gesture. Negatively trained celibates have proved highly incapable of the adjustment to love. They find it incredibly hard to replace mindless conformity with personal responsibility to the God of freedom. Misguided training produced the negative people who could take a vow of poverty without giving, a vow of chastity without loving, a vow of obedience without serving.

Nowhere was celibate training so negative as in the field of chastity. Sex was treated as a rebellious daughter who got herself pregnant, ran off, married outside the Church and was never spoken of again. To all intents and purposes she might never have been born, except that while no one mentioned her name, in her absence she dominated the whole household. She was constantly on everyone's mind, was blamed for all the family unhappiness and especially for everything that happened after she left. The sexual was spoken of, when necessary, in muted tones, and referred to as "lower nature". The implication was that it was both somewhat unworthy of its Creator and a "tiger in the tank" ready to devour anyone who tampered with it. Sex, then, certainly could be accepted fully only by rejecting celibacy. The *strong inclination to evil* resulting from Original Sin, as understood, was unconsciously accepted as referring primarily to sexual sin. Sexual sin took on a horrendous significance that it in fact does not generally have, primarily because, more often than not, it lacks one or two of the necessary qualities for serious sin, namely, full knowledge and full consent. Celibates who suppressed their sexual desires were encouraged to believe that they had supernaturalized them when, in fact, they had merely crippled themselves emotionally.

Celibacy is meaningful when dedicated to leading man to the promised land of the loving life. It should be the free choice of many people who know that man's real troubles came with his refusal to love. Celibates are free, and when they truly love can be the ombudsmen and prophets of mankind, leading the world in the battles for mercy and justice between peoples, races and nations. They can live and act, in the name of God, with such love for one and all that the presence of God is clearly manifest. This is real celibacy, and its work is all ahead of it. It has a relevance today that it never had before. It will bring people forward who inspire the world's losers with hope that they too can find meaning in life. Celibates will inspire a world oriented to pride, greed and sex to see that it really profits a man nothing if he gains the whole world and loses his soul in selfishness and unloving.

They will point out to man that if through faith in himself he has accomplished so much, how much more will he do with faith in the God who began it all, whose terms for happiness are the very same loving which man has consistently rejected, to his eternal shame and corruption.

The new celibate insists that he first of all is a real person who only then can be a celibate. Celibacy is no way of life for fugitive, fearful, part people. The priest's mission, like that of Christ, will depend on his humanity, through which he will show Christ to the world as Christ showed the Father. It must be a healthy, loving humanity. And his celibacy will be accepted in imitation of Christ. It is not simply a physical fact but a truly loving way of life. His love, like all love, takes the emphasis off himself, leaving his great concern for others.

Conclusion

Enjoying leisure, comfort, pleasure and entertainment on a hitherto unknown scale, man still finds happiness remarkably rare. He is surprised by the general reaction to affluence – it is not gratitude but greed. Hunger, poverty, sickness and other basic ills are rather easy to contend with; man, however, is not. He is still THE PROBLEM.

The shrill protests of ecologists and conservationists hardly veil the fact that pollution is not the work of factories but of people, that it is not smoke but selfishness which threatens the balance of nature. It is ridiculous to think of overpopulation as the world's primary problem. That is, in fact, the underpopulation of the world by loving and concerned people. When man cleans up himself he will have made a fine beginning to cleaning up his world.

Man needs to be schooled in loving. He must see and admit that sex is not love, and all too seldom has anything to do with love. Celibate love makes this quite clear. There is nothing about marriage which is necessarily anti-love. But then, there is nothing about either sex or marriage which is essentially loving. Love is not something one falls into naturally, effortlessly, but something achieved after years of learning and practice. Painfully acquired discipline, like patience, always precedes the love which reaches perfection in the single life, in marriage, or in celibacy.

Whatever helps one to love is good; whatever retards the development of the loving person is destructive and bad. Celibacy, genuinely lived, removes many obstacles to deep person-to-person relationships. Thus the celibate's role is as unique as his loving. Certainly, when genuinely given to God and God's people, the celibate's love is inspiring, and his role as teacher extraordinary. Since the perfection of man is love, it requires his best, which is precisely the goal of the real Christian. Spiritually, religious people insist that their purpose in life is Christian perfection. Nothing brings one so close to perfection as loving well. It is an accomplishment worthy of Jesus Christ. Who can doubt that it achieves man's redemption?

When man no longer follows his dominant urge to suck pleasure from the breast of affluence without being compelled to make a spiritual return for his joy, he is redeemed. Man's return to the world for its investment in him will be spiritual when he accepts that love must do more than tickle his palate, stimulate his venereal nerves, fill his eye with beauty or his head with glory; when he understands from experience that love opens the very core of man from which his happiness flows. When love is achieved man has finally evolved, he has become everything that he could ever hope to be, everything he is destined to become. Peace will then be a fact rather than a slogan.

OTHER BOOKS FROM OUR SUNDAY VISITOR

SPEAK LORD
by Rev. John H. McGoey, S.F.M.

Christian hope through Christ's own words is the theme of the book. The author gives fresh insights into Christ's miracles and parables and exciting observations on many personalities in the Gospels. 188 pages, paperbound No. 754 . . . $1.75

TO SETTLE YOUR CONSCIENCE
by Rev. Cass Kucharek

A sensible layman's guide to moral theology. Its sole aim is to be practical in solving the moral problems of everyday life. Using solid Catholic reasoning together with realistic examples, TO SETTLE YOUR CONSCIENCE brings peace to the mind and soul by defining exactly the Church's position on individual acts. It could provide the answer you've been looking for. 264 pages, paperbound No. 877 . . . $3.95

THE TRIAL OF CHRIST
by Rev. Ralph Gorman, C.P.

This reappraisal of Christ's trial and Crucifixion suggests a more reasonable sequence of events in the last hours of Christ's life. Father Gorman takes a critical look at the chronological possibilities and probabilities of Christ's arrest, conviction and execution. 200 pages, paperbound No. 811 . . . $2.95

THOUGHTS ON SUFFERING, SORROW AND DEATH
BY Michael Harrity

Triple polio struck and crippled Mike when he was 21 and a student for the Catholic priesthood. Mike is dead now, but he left a legacy of love, hope, humor and courage. THOUGHTS ON SUFFERING, SORROW AND DEATH is an intensely personal account of those years of sickness and their wonderful meaning. 96 pages, paperbound, No. 812 — $1.95

(continued)

CATHOLIC ALMANAC

    compiled and edited by Rev. Felician A. Foy, O.F.M. The most-complete-one-volume encyclopedia of Catholic facts and information available. It contains accurate statistics on every aspect of Catholicism. Revised and up-dated each year. 704 pages, clothbound No. 871 . . . $9.95, paperbound No. 818 . . . $4.95

WHAT DIFFERENCE DOES JESUS MAKE?

    by Frank J. Sheed

In this age of "Superstar" and "Jesus Rock," young, zealous Christians are knocking on the door of the Establishment with this haunting question. The author answers not with stifled jargon or meaningless rhetoric, but with soul searching dialogue. Using Christ's own words and applying Scripture to life today makes the difference. 242 pages, paperbound No. 810 . . . $2.95

THE CHURCH YESTERDAY AND TODAY

    by Rev. Msgr. John Sheridan

A book to assure and inform those upset by the many "changes" in the Catholic Church today. By applying basic unchanging Church teachings to present day situations, Monsignor Sheridan, in a question and answer format, clears away doubts, misunderstandings and problems for Catholics. 288 pages, paperbound, No. 867 . . . $2.95

If your bookseller does not have these titles, you may order them by sending listed price (we pay postage and handling) to the Book Department at the address below. Enclose check or money order — do not send cash.

Write for free book list
Our Sunday Visitor, Inc. / Noll Plaza / Huntington, IN 46750